WEIGHT LOSS THROUGH YOGA

Jewel in the Lotus

James Donavon Bothell

BOOK PUBLISHERS NETWORK

Bothell, Washington

U.S.A.

Book Publishers Network

P. O. Box 2256

Bothell, WA 98041

425 483-3040

www.bookpublishersnetwork.com

10 9 8 7 6 5 4 3 2 1

LCCN 2012935530

ISBN 978-1-937454-29-6

Editor: Nelda Danz

Design of cover, book and website: Michèle Savelle GIS & Graphic Design

Photography: William Wickett, Michèle Savelle, NASA

Web development: Murray Sampson, Sublime Point Design

Model: Marlow Mercer

Illustrations: Cicelia Wickett (line drawings), Virginia Shaw ("Fish Mandala"),

    Katie Clark ("Beyond Vanity") J.D. Bothell

Audio: Klaus Liebetanz

This book is dedicated to my teacher Marie Svoboda,
and her teacher Sri T. Krishnamacharya.

Mother, father, I share your love.

I see my life come shining
from the west down to the east.
Any day now, any day now,
I shall be released.
Bob Dylan

TABLE OF CONTENTS

INSIDE

There are yoga classes available in most cities and many small towns across the county these days, and countless yoga books and articles have been published. So why write another book about yoga and weight loss?

Consider this scenario, which is not uncommon: an overweight individual attends a yoga class with several participants. He or she bravely tries to do the postures, but the extra weight and steep learning curve make it difficult to keep up with the rest of the class. The instructor has designed the class to accommodate a wide range of abilities, but cannot devote significant individual attention to the struggling student. A yoga practice would likely be very beneficial if the aspiring overweight yogi continued with the classes. However, by the end of the hour, exhaustion and discouragement exceed the rewards, and there is little chance the new yogi will return for another session.

Written with the overweight person in mind, this book provides entry into the full expression of yoga for all.

Compassion, invoked by this conundrum, inspired this book.

Anyone can use yoga as a path for personal transformation. As it is now practiced in the West, yoga is mainly a system of physical exercise. While the physical postures are an important element, they are only a small part of the whole science of well being that yoga offers. Even a person paralyzed with spinal cord injuries can experience the physical, mental, and spiritual metamorphosis that is a result of a sincere, complete yoga practice.

It is rare to meet a serious yoga practitioner with weight problems. Exercise is helpful, but many other factors, some very subtle, help the yogi's body find and maintain its optimum form. The science of yoga is a vast body of knowledge that predates recorded history. This ancient discipline provides a comprehensive framework for understanding our selves and our relationship to the universe. Yoga's wisdom and tools can be used to create a balanced life and fully realize one's potential.

This book isn't just an intellectual exercise. It clearly describes simple actions that can enhance one's ability to objectively assess obstacles to physical health and self-awareness, and to creatively transcend those obstacles. It is written with the overweight person in mind, but the information presented here provides entry into the full expression of yoga for all.

The first section provides a brief overview of the practice, followed by detailed illustrations of a Morning Ritual. This takes only a little time each day, but even a few weeks of daily practice will allow the new yogi to see how quickly one's body can change. Despite all the diet books sold and diets attempted, and despite the use of hypnosis, counseling, gym memberships, personal trainers, drugs, and questionable medical procedures, ever increasing numbers find themselves unable to control their weight. Anyone who has explored these expensive (and often ineffective) options will be relieved to see how little effort is required to see dynamic results, even in the short term. The Morning Ritual takes about thirty minutes to alter the metabolic rate, and it improves one's perspective for the whole day.

The next section offers an understanding of how yoga has come to comprehend the human body, the purpose of life and our place in the universe, as learned through thousands of years of quiet observation. In addition to providing practical actions to alter the body and outlook, the book reveals the philosophy and metaphysics of yoga— connecting Eastern and Western thought and traditions as no other work has done to date. This section also discusses why personal experience is necessary for positive change and why our expectations should be greater than previously imagined.

Once the new yogi has gained a degree of mastery with the Morning Ritual, the next section presents a Ten Minute Yoga Workout to exercise and limber the entire body. Forty-eight flowing yoga postures are demonstrated with detailed descriptions next to them. Once the recommended practice feels familiar, the reader can experiment with additional asanas and other tools, such as mudras. Anyone who becomes comfortable with the daily practice can relax and be confident while doing asanas in a group environment.

The closing sections are transcriptions of the recordings that accompany the book. The first is a dialogue that connects the participant with universal consciousness. The second is an illustrated meditation that summarizes the concepts behind the complete practice.

The reader will
see how little
effort yoga
requires and
quickly starts
to see dynamic
results.

HATHA
BALANCE

HA

Sun
static positive cosmic masculine principle

YOGA
UNION

THA

Moon
active negative cosmic feminine principle

WEIGHT LOSS THROUGH YOGA - JEWEL IN THE LOTUS

Life is learning through experience. Each of us is in the perfect set of circumstances for what it is we should be learning this moment. This includes our body type. Once we've learned the lessons inherent to any circumstance, the lessons change so we can continue learning. Yoga gives us the tools to influence change instead of having the direction of that change be random.

YOGA INSTRUCTION FOR WEIGHT LOSS

A large number of people in our culture are overweight. An even greater portion of society feels dissatisfied, fearful or disillusioned about something in their lives. We carry on but know life could be better. Something is missing. Materialism doesn't fill our cravings; neither will large amounts of food, sex or drugs. What we long for is inside each and every one of us, though it may feel inaccessible. It is our birthright and reason for being.

A beautiful person is in here.

We are all here for a reason, but our culture isn't very good at helping us discover our purpose as individuals. Yoga helps us look inside ourselves to reveal answers to universal questions about living and existence. A sincere yoga practice can relieve suffering and create awareness. Gaining control of our weight is but a small part of the transformation that takes place when we rediscover our bodies, minds and spirits. Permanent weight loss occurs as a side effect of tuning ourselves to the music of creation that we might resonate with the glory of our being.

WHAT'S WRONG?

If you are seriously overweight, your physicality is always the proverbial elephant in the room. Our culture has strong prejudices regarding bodies. People who are heavy not only suffer inconveniences that are the direct result of their size, but they also endure the humiliation of belonging to one of the few groups many think it's all right to tease. A large person faces each day knowing it is going to take extra effort to accomplish many of the day's most mundane functions, and in the background there is also concern, or effort not to be concerned, as to what others are thinking about them because of their size.

A beautiful person is in here. That is one of the truths we all feel. Yoga lets us get in touch with our true self and helps us peel away the layers of unawareness that have clothed us. Where did existence come from and what are we supposed to be doing here? How do we go about doing it? These are basic questions about the human condition regardless of our size. We're all in the same boat, and it can be frightening to slow down enough to face the bad dream we seem to be lost in. Instead, we find distractions that keep us so busy that we can ignore our emotional state. Rather than taking time to understand ourselves, we invent alternative scenarios for our lives: If only I had that lover/could retire/were understood/owned a better car/had a better body. We choose to daydream, not wanting to wake, because without understanding life's most basic fundamentals, life is damn scary. Those who are most successful, even envied, are often are the most lost.

Every aspect of existence is amazing, even miraculous. The heavens, a molecule, a child, a flower–all are astonishing when we stop to consider their essence. What of love, or the fact that you understand the sentences on these pages? Even if we have an intuitive sense of a vast intelligence that creates everything, we may prefer to choose to collect information rather than explore mysteries that could lead to true wisdom. Fear of the unknown may have us running scared, using each other to prop up our individual houses of cards.

Our educations are often reflections of the popular illusions of the day. All through history each civilization has declared its understanding of the world correct and ridiculed the science and medicine of preceding civilizations. The truth is that creation is so vast and intricate we haven't begun to scratch the surface. We only glimpse hints of creation beyond the physical plane. The more scientists learn of the physical universe, the more we realize how little we understand. We know it is wrong, yet we continue to destroy the planet, kill each other, and rob the future. We are making a terrible mess. Is it any wonder some of us wear the weight of this on our bodies?

YOGA

Where did it come from, this yoga that is going to answer all my questions, tune me to the universe, and transform me, body, mind and soul? The historical answer is still a mystery. However, one explanation based on archaeological discoveries is widely accepted. In the 1920's, ruins of a civilization were discovered along a no longer existent river system in the region that is now Northern India and Pakistan. Three thousand years before the birth of Christ, this civilization had complex urban centers with running water and underground sewage systems. Their language, Sanskrit, is the root of all the Indo-European languages.

Among the ruins were found many statues depicting what we now associate as being yoga postures. Postures are a part of the yoga tradition that asks the practitioner to look within. This yoga tradition believes the universe is mirrored in each of us. Nature has a working set of solutions that is used on ever greater or lesser scales for everything, as our recent appreciation of fractals demonstrates. To understand something on a scale within our perceptual range allows us to imagine solutions to questions above or below that range. The yoga postures, asanas in Sanskrit, are only a part of yoga. Yoga as practiced in the West has placed most of its emphasis on the practice of asanas. Most Westerners think of yoga as a system of physical exercise, but it is much more.

Yoga asks us to look within, to relax into our selves, to know ourselves. With complete understanding of the self comes complete understanding. This 'looking within' is as old as the human ability to wonder. In that sense, our origin is the beginning of our embrace of yoga.

One broad definition of yoga is the art and science of living. Yoga practice allows understanding to unfold. Other people may help by suggesting techniques for self-exploration, or how and where to look, but all the insights come from your observations. All the answers are your answers. You diligently explore your own direct experience. No faith is required.

> *As self-awareness grows, weight loss is simply a consequence of the yoga practice.*

YOGA, YOU AND WEIGHT LOSS

A sincere yoga practice affects everything in your life and the lives of those around you. As self-awareness grows, weight loss is simply a consequence of the yoga practice. Activities will be suggested. When you do the activities suggested in this book and observe the results, you will be practicing yoga. Because we are all different, some suggestions will be more applicable to you. Your intuition is your best guide.

Explanations and suggestions are intentionally brief so we can get started as quickly as possible. Before you invest much time, I want you to see that this is going to work. Our outlook and physical form have a remarkable ability to change rapidly. Your being is coiled and ready to spring into new modes of feeling and appearing. If you are diligent and sincere in your efforts, your body will change rapidly, but at a pace that is healthy for you. To begin, you will be given a practice designed to allow you to experience results. Practice with an open mind. Later in the text, there is more explanation of how it works.

If we follow some simple rules, there is no way to do any of this wrong. If something is difficult, just do your best. We're not rewarded for perfection; we're rewarded for sincerity. Don't do anything that doesn't feel safe and right to you. We're all the same in some ways, but each of us is also completely unique. Because All is inside each of us, we know our own path. The more we practice, the more we will learn to trust our instincts and intuitions. You have come to this teaching because you are ready for it. You have, in effect, earned it.

CODEX

We should talk about the yogic worldview a little. Many aspects of modern science are rediscovering some of the concepts yoga revealed long ago. A yoga master sees everything as part of an Absolute, Supreme Awareness, Universal Consciousness. At some point this Absolute shattered into innumerable particles so minute and so broadly dispersed that the individual parts no longer recognize themselves as part of the whole. This mirrors modern science's Big Bang Theory, verified by the Hubble Telescope.

What modern science recognizes in the evolutionary processes of life forms, yoga sees at all levels. Energy turns into matter and matter becomes more complex. Matter aggregates as life forms evolve, until that consciousness finally becomes aware of its origin and the grand process it has experienced. This is where you are at this moment.

Humans have gone through a physical evolution as well as an intellectual evolution. Now we are experiencing a time when the main emphasis is on evolution of the spirit. We are waking up, realizing our true identity as parts of that Absolute. With awareness, we can enter the realm of Universal Consciousness with intent and participate in the creation of reality.

This is a natural process. Along with the natural wisdom within each of us that causes a cell to become a blood cell, a brain to think, an embryo to grow into a human, is the wisdom to reach the next stage of our destiny. Yoga provides the tools to tear down structures that prevent this natural understanding.

Modern science has just come to realize everything is vibration. Physics now views the smallest unit of creation as imperceptible, minute vibrations. The frequency of the vibration determines what that unit is. Certain vibrational groupings result in an electron, others a quark, or a meson, etc. Groupings of these elementary particles form atoms, which combine into molecules, which combine to constitute visible matter. Up and down the scale, all is vibrating. Yoga has always held this view and has an identity for the vibration underlying all creation–OM.

Astronomers observing the effects of gravity on the universe have concluded they have no idea what comprises 96% of what is out there. Unfortunately, they have chosen to name this unknown 'dark matter' and 'dark energy'–although it has no light or dark qualities at all. What these names signify is that science is in the dark when it comes to knowing what the greater part of creation is, even on the physical plane. The same scientists who hypothesize the most basic unit of creation as infinitesimal vibrations, and feel this is the way it must be because it works out mathematically, admit that there must be at least ten dimensions for their theory to work.

It is human nature to pretend we have a strong handle on reality, but truly there is much more going on than what can be seen in the material world. Often, our rigidly held outlook limits our ability to see beyond preconceived notions. In yoga everything is divided in two, purusa and prakriti. Everything we feel, experience and see is real, including our dreams, ideas and fantasies. That which has always been, purusa, is unchanging and will always be.

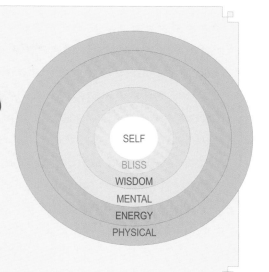

THERE ARE FIVE KOSHAS:

1. A physical body comprised of matter

2. A prana body (Prana is the Sanskrit word for 'life force' that animates all physical and mental activity.)

3. A mental body

4. A knowledge body (knowing beyond sensory perception)

5. An omnipresent, omnipotent, and omniscient body called the bliss body.

Prana, the life force energy, rides the breath.

That is the observer in each of us that even watches our mind think. Everything else is prakriti, impermanent and always in a state of change.

Yoga recognizes our physical body, but also recognizes other bodies, or koshas, occupying the same space as the physical body.

HOW IT'S GOING TO WORK

The popular concepts and solutions dealing with weight loss are concerned with manipulating the physical body by exercising it and denying it food. This can work, but as evidenced by the growing number of overweight persons, it has limited success. We are going to control weight by working with the other koshas. Being too heavy can be thought of as a symptom. Everything is interconnected and this is a holistic approach. We are going to tune our total yogic self. Because we, like all creation, are formed by a multitude of vibrations, tuning ourselves is more than just a metaphor.

Illness occurs when the life force, prana, is obstructed. We are going to clear the obstructions. Think of the body as a furnace. When someone is overweight, the fuel isn't being burned efficiently and keeps adding itself to the mass of the physical body. We all know overweight people who eat like a bird and thin people who eat voraciously. Metabolism can be altered. We are going to do this by relaxing into ourselves; getting in touch with our presently ignored complete self, the self comprised of all our koshas. We're going to turn up the flame. Think of a wood stove with the damper almost closed and the fuel burning all night. With the damper open the same fuel would be consumed in an hour. The flow of prana can be compared to the oxygen allowed to flow by opening the damper.

Yoga recognizes a series of energy centers along the spine called 'chakras'. The chakras exist on the level of the prana body and mirror the endocrine system of the physical body.

The endocrine system controls the metabolism and all body functions using chemical instructions. We are going to direct attention to our chakras. Energy follows attention.

Moving energy can be influenced to form patterns or circuits. The circuits have different qualities such as stimulating, heating, cooling, or relaxing and can be created by touching different parts of the body or holding the body in various shapes. The shapes forming these energy-conducting patterns are called 'mudras'. We are going to employ mudras to stimulate the combustion of stored fuel, fat.

Every day we are going to do a simple series of postures, asanas. We will perform the postures not so much as exercise, but to create awareness, stimulate metabolism and make our bodies more comfortable. We'll also be doing some breathing exercises, called pranayama. These regulated breathing techniques will rev up metabolism and balance body functions.

We are going to look inside and see our bodies as they already exist on a finer plane of reality. Each successive kosha exists on increasingly subtle levels. By focusing attention on ourselves at this more refined level we are going to integrate our present physical manifestation with previously ignored higher elements. Becoming aware of the higher self takes energy. Great amounts of physical energy are utilized in the conversion to spiritual energy. Some of the energy that would be forming our bodies will be sublimated to the creation of awareness.

A subtle process occurs while imaging the self as it is evolving: the process is sped up. On some level we all realize we participate in the creation of reality. As an individual and as a group, we're directing the unfolding of the future with our expectations as well as our actions. No longer are we going to leave everything to the randomness of fate. We are going to familiarize ourselves with our personal path and follow to the ineffable conclusion.

TAKE HEART

The practice we are undertaking isn't going to require tremendous amounts of physical exertion or vast amounts of time. More than anything, it requires sincerity. Only you will know how earnestly you apply yourself, which is perfect, because you are the only person you can't fool.

Everything takes some time to learn, and any new process seems more difficult at first. Do the best you can. More is gained by being sincere in your efforts than by doing it 'right'.

These are skills that everyone can do at some level from the very beginning. They are also very important skills. Compare learning pranayama, asana, or meditation, with learning to play the piano. First you are banging on the keys. With practice, sound evolves into music, and music into mastery. We are fortunate to be learning yoga rather than the piano, because we'll get much more gratification from our most primitive efforts. This is powerful stuff, and with your first attempts, you will start to see results. These activities also have depth. They can be practiced for a lifetime, and if you maintain your awareness, they will continually show you new things. There is no limit to how far you can go. This is the lesson the great sages and religious teachers have been trying to share through the ages. Now is the time for humanity, through you as an individual, to drop the limitations that heretofore have denied our full expression.

There are forces working against your self-realization. First and foremost is your self-image, molded while living at a small percentage of your capacity for so long. When you have a frozen image of yourself, you can't begin to imagine the full extent of your potential. You're locked into old patterns of behavior. Even though they cause you pain, they have the false comfort of familiarity. Others around you may be threatened by your changes. They unconsciously want you to help reinforce their lack of awareness and fear by blindly sharing it. Misery loves company. Once you've gained the strength to share your new awareness, what misery will really love is relief.

You carry everything you need with you everywhere you go.

Also, you'll be experiencing a reality that is beyond what is normal for our culture. There will be doubters, but your own direct experience will be your guide.

Look to physics. When an object is at rest it has inertia, a real force that has to be overcome to start motion. Once you've started, you develop momentum.

THE PRACTICE

The daily practice will take approximately half an hour each morning after you become familiar with the routine. It is important you do it each morning even if ill. If you don't get enough sleep, still get up early enough to do the practice. If, for some reason, you can't do it immediately upon waking, do it as soon thereafter as possible. If by chance you come out of a daydream and realize you've missed a day, get started again right away. This is your chance for a new life.

You don't need much space. On the floor beside the bed, in the kitchen, on the lawn–anywhere there's enough space to lie down flat with your arms and legs spread and stand up with the arms extended above your head will do. A designated space is good, but don't let any little irregularity upset your practice. You don't need any tools. You carry everything you need with you everywhere you go.

Think of the effort and expense people go to: seeing hypnotists, counselors, diet doctors and personal trainers and joining weight loss clubs and gyms. How many diet books are published each year? What invasive, expensive medical procedures are you being offered, and at what risk? Think of the clothing you wear because you are overweight, the opportunities you've missed, and the multitude of daily inconveniences you suffer every hour of every day. Think of the way society would have you feel about yourself if you hadn't already developed an iron will. Yoga is going to work for you, because you are motivated to make it work.

AWARENESS

When you perform your morning ritual, pay attention to what you're doing. Feel your body. Note your breathing. Have your mind on your practice and not on outside distractions. This is the most important time of your day and will determine the quality of everything else you experience in the course of the day.

As the day proceeds there are actions you will do that won't interfere with your activities. Those around you won't even be aware that you are performing them. These actions will increase your awareness and tune your body and mind. You'll be looking into yourself and noticing all the differences the practice makes, and how you are more calm and better organized. You will notice everything from a more balanced perspective. The world will start to become a kinder, more fun place because you are paying attention through the eyes of one who has their priorities right and is on a path to a better life.

Let's begin.

OM MANI PADME HUM

The Jewel in the Lotus

The Buddha of Compassion and his Consort

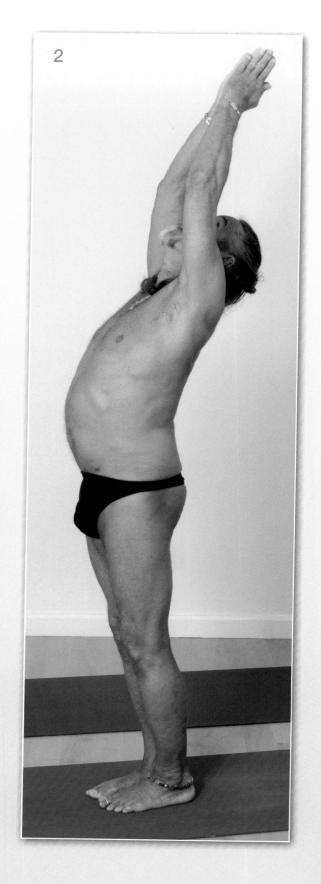

GETTING STARTED

First we'll discuss the morning home practice, step by step. We'll go into the minimum amount of detail to make everything understandable. This is so we can get started as soon as possible. Later we'll go into more depth. After the initial description there will be a very brief and illustrated program you can follow as you actually perform the exercises. The spine of this book is designed to lie flat for convenient reference until the ritual becomes second nature.

A yoga mat can be used, or a rug can be helpful if no mat is handy, but the exercises can be done on a hard floor using something soft like a blanket under the knees.

Traditionally yoga was done facing the East, but the direction you face is of minor importance.

Wear clothing that is comfortable and allows for freedom of movement. Usually, most yogis wear as little as possible.

Unless directed otherwise, you should have eyes open and breathe through the nose.

MORNING HOME PRACTICE

Stand upright with your hands in front of your heart in Prayer Position, feet comfortably apart and facing forward. [Photo 1]

Pause and reflect on four things:

1. Focus on the third eye between and behind the brows.
2. Breathe. Don't hold the breath. Be aware of the breath and breathe into whatever physical sensation gains your attention. Remember, prana, the life force, rides the breath.
3. Be one with your inner teacher, the guru that is in you.
4. Relax, relax, relax, relax.

Breath of Fire

Perform a series of rapid nasal exhalations (twenty four repetitions).

Exhale rapidly through the nose, pulling the belly in sharply with each exhale. The inhale will take care of itself.

Begin the series of asanas (postures) named "Sun Salutation."

Sun Salutation

Still standing with hands in Prayer Position, pause.

Extend the arms straight overhead and touch the palms. Pause and bend back slightly. [Photo 2] Whenever switching arm positions, swing arms down and up in wide arcs.

GETTING STARTED

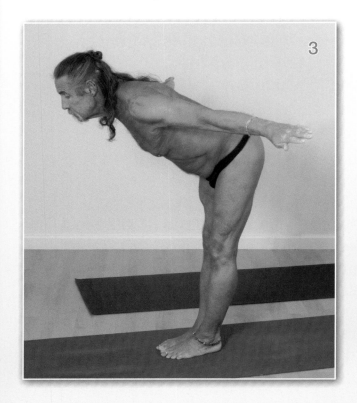

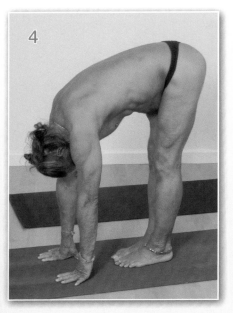

Move into a Forward Bend. Swing arms out and down away from the sides [Photo 3], bending forward at the waist. Bend forward as much as is comfortable. Let head hang and place hands on thighs, knees, shins, feet, or the floor [Photo 4]. Pause a moment with body relaxed and hanging from a bent waist.

Do Extended Forward Bend by straightening your spine parallel to the floor, slightly arching the back and extending through the head [Photo 5] with fingertips on the floor, feet, shins, or thighs depending on your flexibility.

Return to Forward Bend [Photo 6].

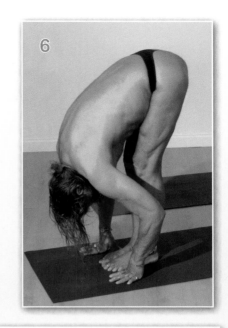

Go into Runner's Lunge by placing both hands on the floor, bending the left knee and extending the right leg straight behind you. Have left foot flat on the floor and have toes bent on the floor behind the extended right leg, like a runner in the starting blocks before a race. (Remember, do what you can, if you have difficulty, know you'll improve with practice.) Hold your back straight; extend through the top of the head and the right heel [Photo 7].

Go into Downward Dog by placing both hands on the floor, shoulder width apart and both feet on the floor, hip width apart. Let head hang and push back from the palms trying to bring the heels down, pushing the tailbone back and up into the air. The distance between hands and feet varies per individual, a greater distance being more challenging. If it is impossible to accomplish with legs straight a first, you can go down to the knees if necessary [Photo 8]. Hands should be flat.

GETTING STARTED

Do Table Top with hands directly below the shoulders, knees below the hips, legs straight back, and toes tucked under. Back, neck, and arms are straight [Photo 9].

Bend elbows slightly and swing chest forward in a low arc [Photo 10]

Let waist drop down and forward, relax the small of the back, and pull chest forward. Look up into Cobra Posture [Photo 11]. Tops of feet lay flat, shoulders roll back creating a curve in the spine. Elbows should be bent and thighs should stay as close to the floor as possible.

Return to Table Top, [Photo 9]

Then go back to Downward Dog. [Photo 8]

Return to Table Top. [Photo 9]

Put the left knee down and swing the right leg forward to Runner's Lunge. [Photo 12]

Do Forward Bend. [Photo 4]

Do Extended Forward Bend. [Photo 5]

Do Forward Bend. [Photo 6]

Do a reverse swan dive to standing with a slight back bend. [Photo 3]

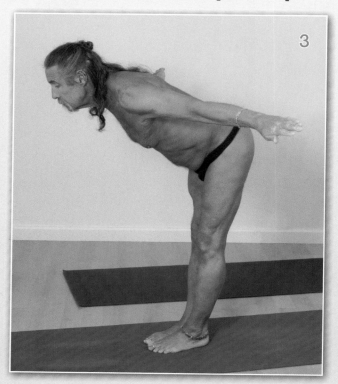

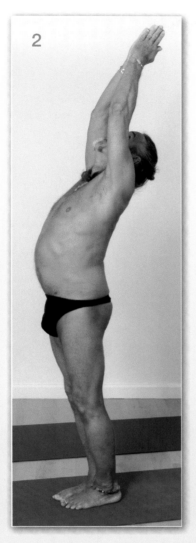

Bring arms together straight overhead. [Photo 2]

Return hands to heart and pause. [Photo 1]

Repeat the whole sequence, but start with the left foot back this time for Runner's Lunge and the right leg bent and forward. When returning to standing at the end of the Sun Salutation, bring the left foot forward in Runner's Lunge. Do four repetitions, both sides, alternating. Do poses at your own pace. Breathing should stay relaxed and even.

Pause.

Stomach Roll

Stand, bending at the waist with hands on the thighs, hands half turned so thumbs are to the outside [Photo 13].

Exhale till lungs feel empty.

Pull in upper right quadrant of the belly, then release and relax.

Pull in upper left quadrant of the belly, release and relax.

Pull in lower left quadrant, release and relax.

Pull in right lower quadrant, release and relax. At first only the slightest movement in the belly may be perceived. This is fine. By paying attention each time, awareness and an energetic connection are being created.

Breathe until breath is normal.

Repeat four times.

Balancing breath

Come to a comfortable sitting position.

Sit with arms crossed over chest, right arm on top, and palms under armpits.

Breathe four complete breaths.

Remove left hand from right armpit and place left arm over right arm with left hand back under right armpit.

Breathe four complete breaths [Photo 14].

Softly close both eyes.

Alternate Nostril Breathing

The Sanskrit word for controlled breathing is pranayama.

Relax left hand on left knee while holding Prithvi, or Grounding Mudra with the left hand. [Photo 15]. Make the Grounding Mudra by holding the top of the thumb lightly touching the top of the ring finger. The other three fingers are extended and relaxed.

Place the three middle fingers of the right hand just between and above the brows [Third Eye or Brow Center] with the thumb on the right nostril and the little finger on the left nostril [Photo 16].

Open and breathe out of the left nostril; close the left nostril, and open

the right nostril. Then breathe in.

Repeat three times.

Switch to breathing out of the right nostril and in the left.

Do three times.

Do full sequence on both sides four times.

Relax and breathe normally.

Meditate

With both eyes closed, and still comfortably seated, place both hands on the knees in Prithvi (Grounding Mudra) [Photo 17] with palms facing down.

Mentally count the length each breath is executed.

Breathe out twice as many counts as you breathe in. For example: out for four counts, in for two counts. Do what's comfortable for you.

After each inhalation, pause for a comfortable moment and suspend the breath.

Do this sequence of out, in and pause for eight cycles on each center of focus. The centers of focus will be the chakras, one at a time, starting at the base of the spine and ascending.

Sitting relaxed, focus your attention on your perineum. The perineum is that part of the anatomy between the legs behind your sex and ahead of the anus. Do your breathing for eight relaxed cycles while feeling grounded to what's below you. With your inner eye picture dark, almost black, the color of extremely rich soil. Feel grounded.

On the eighth exhale, pause and feel the attention (energy) move up the tailbone to the base of the spine. The base of the spine is the general location of the First, or Sacrum Center, Chakra. Focus on the base of the spine and breathe for eight cycles. Relax and feel (be conscious of) a beautiful, brightly oxygenated, blood red.

On the eighth exhale and pause feel attention (energy) move up the spine to below and behind the navel. Be flooded with the color orange. This is the Second, or Navel Center, Chakra.

After the next pranayama (controlled breathing cycle), on the eighth, exhale and pause. Have the attention move to just below the diaphragm, to the Third, or Breath Center, Chakra.

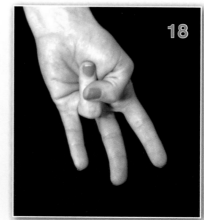

Change hands to Surya Sun Mudra by laying the ring finger across the palm and covering it with the length of the thumb. [Photo 18] Press down slightly on the ring finger with the thumb, pressing firmly into the palm.

Be immersed in the bright yellow of the sun.

Palms are facing up. [Photo 19]

Following the next cycle of eight breaths, move the attention up to the Fourth, or Heart Center, Chakra and flood your consciousness with a beautiful chlorophyll green.

Change hands to Gyan, Peace Mudra, by placing the tips of the index fingers just below the first joint of the thumbs and extending the other fingers in a relaxed manner [Photo 20]. Hands will remain in Peace Mudra with palms facing up for the rest of the chakra meditation.

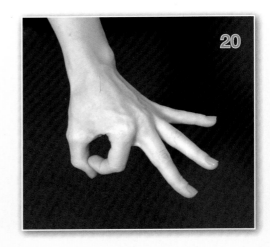

Open the heart in Heart Center meditation [Photo 21] and feel the heart through the back.

After that cycle of pranayama, move your focus to the base of the throat, to the Fifth, or Throat Center, Chakra. Everything is light blue, like a light blue sky.

An eight cycle of pranayama (breathing out twice as many counts as you breathe in, then pausing, as described at the beginning of this section) and then focus about three inches behind and slightly above the brows of the eyes. This is the Sixth, or Brow Center, Chakra and is awash with a deep dark blue, like the night sky on a moonless night.

Another breath cycle and attention floats to the crown of the head, to the Crown Center or Seventh Chakra and consciousness is filled with a bright ultra violet.

After eight exhales, inhales and pauses, consciousness floats above the head and the attention is focused on a beautiful Thousand Petal Lotus (water lily) that is so strikingly pure white, it radiates all the colors of the spectrum.

Do a final eight cycles of pranayama. Realize the lotus starts in the mud at the bottom of the pond, grows up through the muddy water to the surface and opens, a beautiful unblemished white, basking in the sun.

Breathe normally and swing the arms overhead in a wide arc.

Bring the palms together capturing the purity. [Photo 22] Capture the radiant white in your palms.

Then slowly pull your hands down to rest on the crown of the head [Photo 23]. The radiant white mixes with the ultra violet. The elbows are extended wide.

With palms together in Prayer Position, move them down and touch the forehead in front of the Brow Center, with elbows together. [Photo 24] Pause and feel the dark blue combine with the light from above.

Move them down to the Throat Center, elbows wide, and pause. [Photo 25] The colors from above blend with the light blue.

Then lower the prayer position palms to the Heart Center, elbows relaxed at your sides, and pause, feeling the green merge with the radiance from above. [Photo 26]

While holding the hands together in Prayer Position over the heart, let the attention float to the Breath Center and experience the yellow mixing.

Then to the Navel Center, where the orange combines.

Next, attention shifts to the sacrum, where red blends, intermingling all the colors of the spectrum.

Then to the perineum and below.

Feel the energy moving in waves up from below and through the top of the head and beyond. Know waves don't really advance, but undulate giving the appearance of upward movement.

Allow the consciousness to gather again in the Heart Center. From here, your heart, you will face the world.

Inhale slowly and voice a long 'OM'.

Do this three times. 'OM' has five components, the 'ah', the 'oh', and the 'um', plus the vibration of the throat and lips, and the stillness of the mouth, throat and lips. The sound starts at the back of the throat and slowly moves forward to the closing of the mouth and the vibration of the lips.

After three long OMs, with hands still in Prayer, move palms back up to the Third Eye Center [Photo 24] and say out loud, "The Divine in me recognizes the Divine in you and in All."

Return palms in Prayer to the Heart Center and speak out loud, "Namaste." [Photo 26]

Bow forward.

Relax and pause in Seated Prostration [Photo 27] and reflect.

Return to Seated Prayer Position and pause. [Photo 28]

This finishes the morning home practice for the day.

It can be done very quickly after you've become familiar with the ritual. Always stay awake and aware of what you're doing and it will have a new richness each time. If you are completely distracted and feel you are just going through the motions, don't be disheartened. The practice will still be effective. By performing the practice, you are stimulating internal triggers that are setting off a cascading series of energetic events. Even so, try not to become robotic in your practice. Mechanization is a part of what prevents us from realizing our full self, from experiencing the freshness of each of life's moments. The practice is a joy. Be grateful you can turn up awareness of every aspect of your being. The time and effort you are spending will be rewarded many times over in greater efficiency and will enhance every moment of your day.

Observances to do in the course of the day

Do the Suyra (Sun Mudra) with one or both hands whenever convenient. [Photo 18] This will create heat and change the metabolism, consuming the body as fuel and will also stimulate awareness. Be sure to drink a lot of water to stay hydrated.

When you think about it, breathe the "exhale twice as long as inhale, then pause" pranayama. This will center and relax you while altering your metabolism. You'll feel the effects.

When you go to bed, lie on your back and consciously relax. Feel the energy of the Pranayama Body (Energy Body) within your Physical Body. Visualize it as light. Be aware of your whole being. Feel the Energy Body pulsating with life force and connected to the energy of the universe. Reflect on the satisfaction you feel having done your morning practice and having maintained a higher state of awareness through the day. Reflect on the new insights that are arousing you from unconsciousness. Fall into slumber seeing the person you want to be and know you truly are. Relax into that more perfect self that already exists within you. Feel the many ways your day was enriched by your expanded awareness. Relax into your true self and feel that self here now. Know that as you sleep everything is getting better.

....

The next section is a condensed guide to the morning home practice, an illustrated summary for quick reference until the routine is put to memory.

DAILY MORNING RITUAL

Stand with hands in Namaste (prayer)

Focus on the third eye between the brows.

Breathe; be aware of the breath and breathe into sensation.

I am one with the guru, both inner and outer.

Relax, relax, relax, and relax.

Breath of Fire

Twenty-four rapid nasal exhalations while pulling in the belly

Sun Salutation sequence

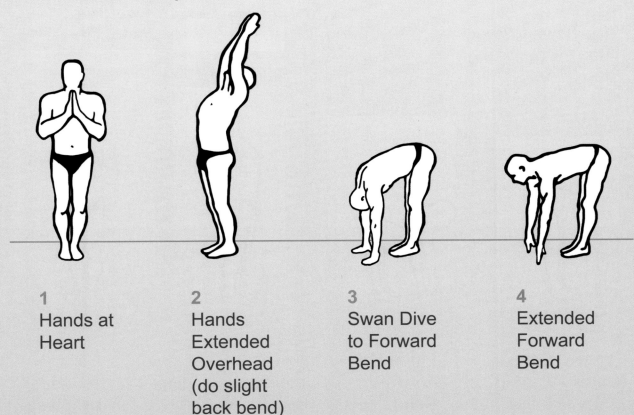

1
Hands at
Heart

2
Hands
Extended
Overhead
(do slight
back bend)

3
Swan Dive
to Forward
Bend

4
Extended
Forward
Bend

5
Runners
Lunge
(right side)

6
Downward
Dog

7
Table Top

8
Cobra
(go down to knees
and swing through
to…)

9
Table Top
(return to…)

10
Downward Dog
(return to…)

11
Forward Bend
(walk forward to…)

12
Extended
Forward
Bend

13
Reverse Swan Dive
(come to standing,
with backbend)

14
Hands
at Heart
(Namaste)

Repeat sequence beginning with the left foot back. Do the entire sequence (both sides) four times.

Stomach Roll

Stand.
Bend at the waist, knees slightly bent and hands on the tops of thighs.
Exhale and pull in right upper quadrant of the belly and relax.
Pull in the left upper quadrant of the belly and relax.
Pull in the lower left quadrant and relax.
Pull in the lower right quadrant and relax.
Let your breath return to normal, then repeat the sequence 4 times.

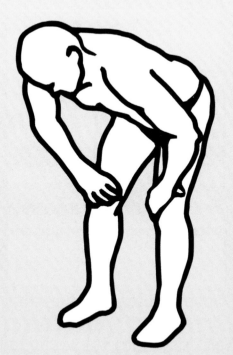

Balancing Breath

Sit.
Cross arms at the chest with the right arm on top and both hands under the arms in the armpits.
Take four relaxed breaths.
Switch, bringing left arm to the top.
Take relaxed four breaths.

Alternate Nostril Breathing sequence

The three middle fingers of the right hand are placed over the Third Eye.
The thumb is placed on the right nostril.
The little finger is placed on the left nostril.
Open and exhale through the left nostril.
Close the left and open the right nostril.
Inhale.
Repeat three times, then switch, exhaling right and inhaling left.
Do full sequence, both sides, four times.

Breathe normally and relax.

Meditation sequence

Sit with legs crossed, hold hands in Grounding (Prithvi) Mudra. Breathe out twice as many counts as you breathe in. Pause briefly (whatever is comfortable) after you inhale.

Complete eight cycles of breathing for each center of focus (chakra).

Focus on the perineum—feel grounded.

Feel the energy move up to the base of the spine (eight breath cycles)—feel the color red.

Focus behind the navel (eight breath cycles)—feel orange.

Focus behind the diaphragm (eight breath cycles)—feel yellow.

Form Sun (Surya) Mudra.

Focus at the heart center (eight breath cycles)—feel green.

Form Peace (Gyan) Mudra and hold to end of meditation.

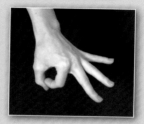

Focus on the base of the throat (eight breath cycles)—feel light blue.

Focus behind the brow center (eight breath cycles)—feel indigo blue.

Focus on the crown of the head (eight breath cycles)–feel a skullcap of ultra violet.

Let attention float above the head (eight breath cycles)–feel a thousand-petalled white lotus radiating highlights of all the colors.

Open the arms in a wide arc, swinging up to meet in prayer with arms extended overhead.

Place hands in prayer position over the crown of the head with elbows out.

Place hands in prayer position over the brow center with elbows together.

Place hands over throat center with elbows wide.

Place hands over heart center with elbows relaxed.

Focus on the diaphragm and Breath Center, then move your attention down the spine: the Navel Center, the Sacrum (spine) Center; the region below the perineum.

Picture a shaft of energy extending 40 feet above you, running down through your spine, and then 40 feet below you.

See your heart as the center of this shaft, radiating beautiful green light.

Interact with the world from your heart.

Inhale and slowly voice a long 'OM'. Do this three times.

Place the hands in prayer over the third eye again and audibly say, "The Divine in me recognizes the Divine in you and in all."

Place the hands in prayer back over the heart and say, "Namaste."

Bow forward at the waist.

"The Fish Mandola"
Virginia Sept. 2005

GOING DEEPER

You are being diligent with your morning home practice. When possible, you are performing the Suyra Mudra and the 'exhale twice as long as inhale and pause' pranayama. You know the satisfaction of taking control and doing something about your weight, and, more important, changing your life. From your first efforts, you can see the practice is making a difference.

Already your intuition recognizes this path. Your time is now and your spirit is alert to the many subtle changes going on within your body, your outlook, and the way the world regards you.

In the beginning, it is not easy. You have to put forth the extra effort it takes to overcome inertia and form new routines. You may feel sore from exerting previously unused muscles. Others might question what you're doing. Don't feel you have to explain yourself to others. You can draw on the satisfaction that you are making a difference in your life. Just enjoy it when others notice something life changing is happening with you.

There is a natural intelligence guiding everything.

It may seem like a lot of work at first. It takes a lot of attention. Be cognizant your focus is nurturing a new self-awareness. You are beginning to swim up out of the whirlpool of worries and mental chatter that used to dominate your mind. Look inside and feel your true nature gaining strength. Every time something occurs and you react in a new way and realize it is different than the way you would have reacted before, give yourself a pat on the back.

Know everything is in a constant state of flux. The one thing you can always count on is change. You never put your foot down in the same stream. We've been conditioned to resist change, to hold on to what we've got. This is an expression of fear of the unknown. When we know so little, it can be a very frightening proposition. Understand that the ego driven self knows very little, but there is a natural intelligence that is guiding everything. Embrace change. Think of it as the road to liberation. Know things are unfolding as they should, and that there is a grand design.

DO YOU MIND

Our Western culture has come to regard our minds as 'us'. Our minds are wonderful and amazing. In order for humans to survive, to give us time to evolve, we had to make sense of our environment. Our minds sorted out the information deemed necessary for survival, a minute portion of our sensory input. The vast majority of stimulus is ignored.

Add to that filtering of information the knowledge that we're designed to register only a narrow band of the wavelengths undulating in the dance of creation, and we realize our minds have made extremely large assumptions based on very little information. Given our success as a species, our limited minds have done an amazing job. In some regards, perhaps we have accomplished too much.

YOGA REVERES BALANCE

If the earth were a little closer or further away from the sun, if the moon wasn't balanced in orbit acting as a stabilizer, the planet wouldn't have been able to foster consciousness in this human form. An intricate balance of hot and cold gasses, liquids and solids form this womb, Mother Earth.

The human body is a finely tuned, finely balanced vessel for awareness. Multitudes of balanced chemical and functional relationships are requisite for our being. Just as the earth revolves in its perfect orbit without the coaching of our minds, so our infinitely complicated bodies draw upon a higher order. Our bodies are always working to maintain a proper relationship among the gases, liquids and solids animated by the life force into a living organism. This sacrosanct coalesce is constantly going on without direction from our thinking mind.

> *The mind is notified of an imbalance and the thought 'hunger' arises.*

If the body registers the need for hydration, it signals the mind, which generates the thought, "I'm thirsty." The mind went about a set of actions to get water into the body to reestablish balance. The same process happens with fuel. The mind is notified of an imbalance and the thought 'hunger' arises. The necessary step to maintain equilibrium, ingestion of food, follows. Often this cycle isn't immediate. Our ancestors spent a lot of their time feeling hunger. The clever mind learned to eat more than was necessary to forestall the immediate craving, storing fuel on the body as fat. A mental association with overeating and a feeling of security and wellbeing was established. Now many of us, especially in the United States where food is so abundant and inexpensive, have plenty to eat, but the association with over consumption of food and wellbeing persists.

Our success as a species is largely due to our intelligence, our capacity for thought. The mind has become very good at what it does. Success has spurred it on to greater aspirations. Now it is wonders if it would be better off on its own, and teases itself with notions of a virtual reality. The mind entertains itself with imaginings of 'everything' just being thought. It forgets the requisite coalescence that allows it to exist, making consciousness and thought possible. To state it mildly, the mind has thought itself into a state of imbalance.

The mind has assumed functions that operated perfectly well on their own, coming to think of itself as the being rather than as a part of the being. This takes a vast degree of delusion. Because the inflated status lacks truth, the mind is extremely insecure. It's like the used car salesman that keeps talking fast, pointing out the good features on the car, diverting you from looking under the hood to see the oil leaking.

The mind no longer waits and listens to signals from the body. It sets up schedules for eating. Eating can be a pleasurable activity, so why not eat for pleasure and disregard hunger's cessation? Indulge those primitive associations with security and wellbeing.

If the mind thinks it is everything, it feels it has responsibility for everything. It might not have all the answers, but it knows a lot of diversions. Eating can become one of those diversions. You're feeling out of harmony: how about some crackers? Why not entertain a sexual fantasy and for a few moments you'll forget that nothing seems to have equilibrium? Maybe a television program, or a daydream can obscure the imbalance.

> *The mind becomes quiet enough ... to listen to the body*

The more the mind practices deceit, the more habitual it gets. Of course the diversion never fully works. Eventually you're left sitting in Mobile with the Memphis blues again.

ESTABLISHING BALANCE

Balance is the natural order, so if you are aware of the problem, it can be corrected. You are aware of the problem.

The first step is to relax. When we pay attention to the whole picture, the mind recedes to a proper stature. You aren't your mind and you are in control. When we don't know any better, it is easy to establish bad habits. Now we know better and the situation is already starting to correct itself. The mind is going to help us to reestablish balance. It is looking for something meaningful to do and is tired of the responsibility and deceit.

The mind will do what it can to regain equilibrium, but despite its overblown aspirations, the mind is very limited in its abilities. It does what it can do very well, but it can't do what it is not designed for. You have to keep a close eye on it for a while. Habits need to be broken and new patterns established. As the observer, pay attention to your internal dialogue. Observe moments of quiet, the space between thoughts. Relax into these moments. The mind doesn't have to be going all the time like some radio with no off switch. Don't try to control the mind. Observe it. You'll probably find it entertaining–even comical–in its pretense. You don't have to pay attention for very long before you start to see the mind as a performer, trying to keep everyone's attention without enough dialogue. The same material gets used over and over again. Like an accomplished entertainer, the mind wants you emotionally involved in the production. Observed for a while, the repetition gets boring. You lose interest and let it go 'stage left'.

When the mind is afforded its proper stature, it becomes quiet enough to listen to your body. You can pay attention to the body as it signals its needs. For awhile the mind still voices its wants, but the observer knows that clamoring serves no practical purpose. You see the desire for what it is, an inappropriate solution to a situation that no longer exists. Habitual thoughts of nonexistent hungers can be likened to a sheep dog constantly wanting you to throw the ball so it can fetch. Persistent though the dog is, if you ignore it long enough, it eventually realizes the game is over.

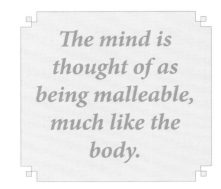

The mind is thought of as being malleable, much like the body.

PRESENT

When your kindergarten teacher called the roll, you would answer, "Present". I'm here now. That's the ideal–to be here now, in the present. This sounds obvious, but many of us rarely have our consciousness in the present. We float through imagined scenarios of the future or reconstructions of a remembered past. This is a tactic the mind employs in an attempt to stay center stage. It is living in a waking dream, better described as never being fully awake. With your consciousness focused on holograms in your head, you're paying less attention to the real world around you. Of course this makes you less efficient because you are basing decisions on an even narrower range of real perceptions. Because you are inside your own mind, you are not in the real world where everything else is, including the objective observer. With everything out here, why hide in that little cranium?

NOW, WHERE AM I?

Western thought developed regarding the mind and spirit (or soul) as being somehow interconnected. Descartes' "I think, therefore I am" is the foundation of Western philosophy.

Eastern philosophy sees the body, mind and spirit as distinct things. The mind is thought of as being malleable, much like the body. The mind needs to be nurtured, but also controlled. The observer, that part of you that watches the mind think and the body function, is the proper seat for consciousness. The observer is purusa: unchanging. It has always been, and will always be. The mind, like the body, is always changing and is impermanent. The mind is prakriti.

Like the body, the mind registers the change it is experiencing. It can feel good and it can feel bad. The observer feels nothing. It just is. It observes what the mind and body are experiencing, but is separate. This is a technique the yogi employs for pain management. Not just severe pain, but the multitude of mental and physical sensations that otherwise cause discomfort. This concept is expressed in the saying "the yogi feels cold, but the yogi doesn't feel cold".

Your proper home is in this higher consciousness, observer consciousness. When you reside here, your being is in its natural home and balanced. Consider the homonyms 'I' and 'eye' and you see that this understanding of the proper seat of consciousness is coded into our language.

If the observer consciousness is you and it always has been and will always be, what's the logical implication?

REINCARNATION

After meditating for a while and getting more acquainted with your complete self, many things are going to start to become clear. Living fully in all of your koshas will facilitate a new form of understanding. The knowledge body kosha knows beyond sensory perception. What existed as concepts or murky theories suddenly becomes obvious. To the yogi, the highest form of thought is 'intuitive', but beyond the way the word is commonly used to describe having a 'hunch'. In this context, intuition is an absolute understanding that just is. Suddenly it is so obvious, you wonder how you didn't always have this understanding. Then you realize, of course, a part of you (your higher self) always did understand, but you didn't consciously inhabit that part of the self. Now your increased awareness simply sees and knows.

Reincarnation is one of these truths.

For 200 years after Jesus, it is estimated that half of the followers of his teachings, Gnostic Christians, believed in reincarnation. The Roman Church, consolidating control over the Christians living in the vast Roman Empire, discouraged this belief. They determined it incompatible with the doctrine of the new religion, and systematically destroyed chapters of the Bible discussing reincarnation.

The Gnostic Christians also believed each individual came to knowledge of God through his own direct experience. They believed this was the very essence of the teaching. In Greek, 'Gnosis' means knowledge. Gnostic Christianity was experiential like yoga. Each person verified the teaching for their self. The Roman Church wanted the priesthood as an authority between God and man. This gave them control and made Rome the center of spiritual knowledge. The modern teaching of Christianity descended from this tradition.

When death isn't final, a lot of fear is removed. If you want to maintain control over others, fear is a powerful tool.

The Celtic culture that dominated what is now Europe north of the Mediterranean before the Christian era also believed in reincarnation. They believed we lived in another world after death waiting to start a new life. The Roman and Greek historical documentarians of the time attributed the Celts' bravery in battle, in part, to this belief.

The most influential spiritual teachers have avoided much discussion of what happens after death. Their focus has been on what to do when alive. A condition inherent to spiritual knowledge is its availability on a need to know basis. Attention is better kept on what will benefit now.

Upon historical examination, where records exist, most of the "pie in the sky" or "hanging over hell on a thread" drama was added on to the teaching by later revisionists. Attempting to advance humanity, teachers saw wisdom in revealing what was most critical for the masses to know to make a reasonable amount of spiritual progress. They had to take into consideration who their acolytes were and what they could understand. This is why, for instance, Jesus speaks of God as the Father, himself as the Son, and humankind as brothers and sisters. This is language and imagery people of that time could understand. Talk of sheep and shepherds was relative culturally. Currently we are using 'god' or 'God' as a way of thinking and talking about matters that are beyond our capacity to understand intellectually. A principle comes into play where beings can't comprehend above their own level of spiritual development. They don't yet perceive on that fine a vibrational level.

Another era has started. Everything that transpired previously was necessary. We are ready. Our cosmic outlook, understanding of science and nature, melding of worldwide cultural insights has made us ready to understand. Previously only a few advanced souls could comprehend. Now everyone who has read this far, and understands what they've read, has the personal tools to utilize the practice to gaze inward and know.

IGNORANCE VS. BLISS

Have you ever watched a child with a severe disability and felt the almost unbearable tragedy? The unfairness can make you feel guilty for being healthy. If this is the only chance at life the child has, it is no chance at all. Ask a minister, "What kind of god does this and why?" "Why are some born in a rich country with everything and others in abject poverty?" "Where is the fairness?" Expressions like "it's God's way" and "life isn't fair" are empty, and not acceptable to the yogi.

Yoga reveres balance and unfairness is a form of imbalance.

If this disabled life is just one of many lives, lives that once they are over almost seem they haven't existed and are soon forgotten, like a dream is quickly forgotten, balance comes through innumerable incarnations, providing a perfect unfolding to teach what we are here to be learning. Each life is fleeting against the backdrop of eternity. All of us start at the beginning and earn advancement to higher more pleasurable incarnations. This seems fair and balanced. What value a god cruel and unfair?

Another principle: the more aware you are spiritually, the fewer rules you have to follow. Imagine a person at a lower level of spiritual understanding, for example, born a serf in Czarist Russia in 1900. Born into a strong patriarchal society, life controlled by the landholder, his trust for an understanding of life in the hands of the Orthodox Church and his national security at the whims of the monarchy. He works like a slave until his early teens and is then sent to the front in World War 1 to be killed in the opening moments of the first meaningless battle. The noble fool followed all the rules to the very best of his ability.

> *Yoga reveres balance, and unfairness is a form of imbalance.*

The other side of this coin: you have to follow fewer rules, but it becomes ever more important you observe the rules you still have. When you have fewer, heavier, objects on a scale, the misplacement of one of those objects makes a greater difference. As we become more aware we see the meaning of things for ourselves and are no longer flotsam swept around by events that have no relevancy to our goals.

Lightness of being is mirrored in the natural world. Solids are dense, rigid and confined in shape, following more rules. Liquids seek their own level and are fluid. Gasses are less dense, volatile, follow the least rules, and they disperse to fill available space. An unselfish motive for following the practice and looking inside and becoming companion to your more subtle, finer self, a more realized being's awareness is volatile, and fosters greater empathy.

The simple fact is, the more you realize your true self, closer you are, using the current verbal shorthand, to God. The closer you are to God the better everything is. This may seem obvious, but spiritual teachers have repeatedly taught this truth with most people still missing the point. A way to know if you are on the right path, in balance with the universe, is whether it feels good–for the long term, not the fleeting pleasure of a beer or candy bar. The finest, most subtle kosha is the bliss body.

NEXT PLEASE

When we die the energy of the life force leaves the body. The physical body reverts back to the earth, water, gas and space from which it was formed. The mental body no longer has the circuitry or energy that made 'it' possible. As a construct of the mental body, the ego no longer exists. Anyone holding a dead being in their arms realizes that consciousness, the spirit, has left. Nobody is home.

The higher koshas have gone somewhere else. The more of you invested in the higher koshas, the more of your being goes with them. When we lose our ego, we don't lose our true identity. The ego is all those things you've been told you are since birth. Our true identity is what has always been uniquely you plus the awareness you've gained through your own direct experience.

As an individual grows closer to their full self through lifetimes of greater awareness, there is more of 'them' carried to the next manifestation. This is why Jesus taught not to squander your wealth (life) on earthly things. When you carry more of your awareness into the next life, you remember what it is you are doing here more quickly and don't waste time casting around trying to figure out what the hell is going on. Before a being reaches a certain development, he or she can spend lifetimes wondering what it's all about.

GROUNDED

What you are now is the accumulation of all you've experienced. Your culture, family history, genetic makeup, education and religious training, plus the influence of all your past lives, form the unique you. Your triumphs and failures are all necessary to the person you are right now. Accept them. Perhaps you have heard the saying, "You can't do the work until you've forgiven your parents." We have to take full responsibility for our selves, unpleasantness and all. Everyone has terrible things happen. That is the nature of existence. Yoga relieves suffering; it doesn't make it go completely away. Yoga changes our perspective so we appreciate the temporary nature of everything. This makes us less vulnerable, more resilient.

There is no need to reject the concepts, insights and language of your previous spiritual training. We're not starting over; we are adding new awareness to our previous state of mind.

When writing, assumptions are made, and the assumed main audience for this writing is Westerners of a Judeo Christian background. The way we express ideas and the examples we use stem from this background. No apology is needed– we have to agree on a common language.

There are many paths. Mankind has been working on trying to make things better for a long time. This is part of our beauty. We strive for betterment, knowing the most effective action we can take overall is to improve ourselves, and that is our most unselfish act. What we now call yogis, in the past came from all sorts of backgrounds. Looking inward to 'see' has been the preoccupation of a few down through the ages. Shamans, saints and witches; mystics and hermits; alchemists and Sufis; parsons and eccentrics–these are just some of the labels for what we are referring to as yogis. Teachers and leaders have

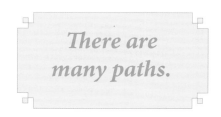

There are many paths.

come forth throughout human history. The common thread is that these individuals looked deeper than their contemporaries did and tried to share what they saw.

It happens that at this time the torch of this introspection has been passed to us from Asia by yogis coming from the Hindu tradition. Much of the ritual and imagery reflect this influence and can be quite effective symbolism. A lot of it is pure nonsense. After religious traditions have been around for a long time, they tend to stray from the purity of the original teaching. The teaching is augmented for personal or political motives. If a story is told enough and only changed slightly with each telling, before long it will only slightly resemble the original story. Sometimes the meaning or intent will change by 180 degrees.

A good example is the caste system in India, in which the group, or caste, a person is born into determines their status. Although it is no longer a legal system, it still holds immense cultural power: the Brahmin, or priest caste, is on top, followed by the warrior caste and then following a descending scale to the lower castes. The bottom castes are so demeaned that they are considered untouchables. This inequity [imbalance] is justified using a misunderstanding of the concept of karma.

At some point in the distant past, yogis noticed different souls learn spiritual lessons in different ways. Some examined reality by keeping track of the tradition around transformation and examined natural processes through the lens of religion. People with this tendency dominant were referred to as priests. Others examined and learned best through confrontation, these souls were grouped as warriors. Others advanced spiritually by teaching and were grouped under the title sage. Several other groupings were recognized, the largest of which was labeled servants because they advanced spiritually through service to others. The yogis noticed the servant grouping, in general, were the most efficient at spiritual transformation. Ironically, those souls who would have made up this grouping are the models for what are now considered the lowest classes in the caste system.

Through introspection, you can find countless examples of this kind of incorrect information distributed under the name of religion. This is why the yogi is above religion. Experience for the yogi is fresh. Each lesson is learned for the first time, pure and undiluted by doctrine. The yogi is grounded in direct experience.

JUST ENOUGH

At humanity's present stage of development, with so much emphasis on the mind, it is easy to place too much value on intellect. Much so-called knowledge (with little or no validity) exists. It is easy to be absorbed by one tangent or another, spending a lifetime becoming expert at something which is not necessarily based on truth. Consider the stereotype of the genius who can't perform basic life skills. We want to be balanced in our person. We only have to know so much, but we need to understand our place and function in the universe and how to enjoy going about it. Along came yoga.

The asana practice came to the West first, and that created a desire to know more about yoga. There can be a lot to learn. Many different schools have been established, promoting various insights. Within the yoga experience there are many paths. It's helpful to be shown techniques, but often the seeker is lulled into someone else's direction. The goal of the truly selfless teacher is to be fired. Everything we need to know is inside us. A lot of time can be wasted on other peoples' programs and chasing someone else's goals. This 'All' is very simple. Looking within and staying in observer consciousness, you only have to know so much. Dogma and doctrine can lure one into ossification. Just because we think of ourselves doing yoga, it doesn't mean we can't fall back asleep.

Be your own guru. No one is going to teach you anything meaningful you don't already understand. Don't close your mind to outside ideas, but remember 'All' has to be experienced directly by you. Be open, but be skeptical. Stay awake!

PARADOX

The *Bhagavad Gita* lays out the yogic world view in the form of a tale of a prince, Arjuna, reluctantly facing battle. A manifestation of the godhead in the form of Krishna, acting as Arjuna's chariot driver, explains why things appear as they do. Arjuna says to Krishna, "My mind is in confusion because in thy words I find contradictions".

As you become more your self and see through your own eyes, the phenomenon of paradox becomes more prevalent. You exercise free will, but recognize a grand design and destiny. Things are the way they are supposed to be this moment, but they should be better.

This is a higher level of understanding. The world is trying to pin things down, but you perceive different strata of reality. Light can be both a wave and a pulse. Different dimensions have different rules. We can live in the same world, the physical universe, but, depending on our level of spiritual development, we experience different realities. Many teachers, Jesus as an example, perform what seem miracles, manifestations of a deeper awareness of the natural order. They tell us this is our birthright, to gain this greater awareness.

IT'S NICE, COME ON IN

You have completed the asana portion of your morning practice and have found a comfortable seat. The left is hand forming the Surya Mudra lying relaxed on your left knee. The right hand is in front of the face with the three middle fingers on the Third Eye, or Brow Center, between and slightly above the eyebrows. The thumb is on the right nostril and the little finger, the left nostril.

Begin Alternate Nostril Breathing

Close the right nostril with a slight pressure of the thumb and breathe out slowly through the left.

Release pressure with the thumb, letting the right side open while applying slight pressure on the left nostril with the little finger, breathing in through the right nostril.

Repeat this sequence of movements and breath three times.

Then Do The Opposite, Or Mirror Image

Close the left nostril with a slight pressure of the little finger and breathe out slowly through the right.

Release pressure with the little finger, letting the left side open while applying slight pressure on the right nostril with the thumb and inhale through the left nostril.

Repeat this sequence of movement and breath three times.

The mudra created with the right hand over the brow center brings attention there and draws energy to the third eye, the seat of awareness. The middle finger is directly over the third eye with two fingers to each side, creating balance. The spinal cord runs from the brain down through the center of the core of the physical body to the sacrum, or lower back.

The nerve tissue of the brain, spine, and complex network of ganglia radiating out through the extremities are animated by prana, the life force, to receive stimulus and transmit, analyze, sort and store the multifarious sensory input received each moment. Just as there is a visible physical system made up of the elements of space, fire, water and earth which forms the physical body and is utilized by the mental body; the prana body has a distribution system, posited in the psyche, for the life force energy. This system is on a more subtle level and can't be seen by the physical eye, but it can be felt when relaxed and perceived with the third eye, which also exists on a finer, more subtle level. Because you are using the nerves of the physical body to feel awareness of the prana body, it can seem to have the form of the nervous system, but it actually extends though the whole living body beyond the reach of the nervous system. Wherever there is life in the physical body, the prana body is what animates that life. The prana body is similar to the nervous system in that it has a main trunk, existing in the same space as the brain and spinal cord, and then radiating or branching out on smaller conduits to the far reaches of the body. Through this system, energy is distributed. The energy should flow freely without obstruction.

When energy flow is impeded, imbalance is created. At the very least, interruption in the flow of energy deprives a part of the body of proper function.

The imbalance creates 'dis-ease', a lack of ease, often sustained for so long the discomfort becomes accepted as a normal part of existence. If sustained long enough, it is the cause of disease.

The recognition of the energy body and the necessity for life force, or 'chi' in Chinese medicine, to flow freely for a person to be healthy is the basic philosophy behind acupuncture. Western medicine acknowledges that acupuncture works, but cannot explain why it works. This is because Western medicine has yet to recognize the koshas and acknowledge the prana body. The acupuncturist is using needles to clear the pathway so the life force can properly flow, restoring balance.

BE NADI

In Sanskrit the junctions energy transverses are called nadis. The largest nadis are located along the length of the spine, running through the energetic centers we've been referring to as chakras, the seven chakras we focused our attention on during meditation. When a human embryo is forming in the womb, the first structure to start developing is the cerebral-spinal region synchronic to the chakras. They are, in ascending order:

1. The base of the spine, the sacrum center
2. Slightly below and behind the navel, the navel center
3. In front of the spine and slightly below the diaphragm, the breath center
4. At the heart, the heart center
5. At the base of the throat, the throat center
6. Slightly above and behind the center of the brows, the brow or third eye center
7. Inside the crown of the head, the crown center.

In the physical body, nerve ganglia known as 'plexuses' have similar roles and positions along the spine. Branching plexuses encircle the endocrine glands and organs, complementing the subtle chakra nadis.

In addition, there are many hundreds of thousands of nadis of varying size and importance wherever pranic energy flows through the body. In Sanskrit 'nadi' means 'stream', denoting the channels the life force navigates. In acupuncture, the pranic energy nadis are referred to as meridians.

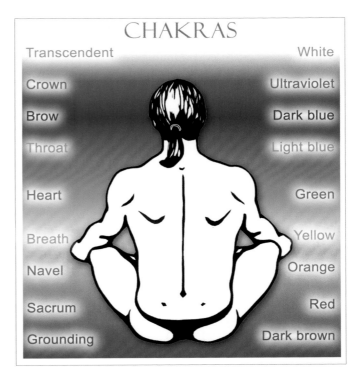

ENDOCRINE SYSTEM

The locations of the seven chakras of the prana body mirror the location of the physical organs of the body's endocrine system, the ductless glands that control the body's functioning through chemical secretions. To permanently adjust our weight to what nature knows is our optimum, we are going to become familiar with each chakra. Through focus and awareness we are going to energize and clear each chakra in turn, gradually opening them to the free flow of prana. Then, we heal and balance each ductless gland affected by each chakra and correct the chemical instructions being released, adjusting those chemicals to instruct the body to be a healthy weight. The body knows how to do this and is anxious to get started. It simply needs the obstructions removed.

1. The first chakra, the sacrum center, is analogous to the ovaries and testicles, producers of female and male reproductive hormones.

2. The second, or navel, chakra mirrors the pancreas, which produces hormones (insulin, glucogen and others) and digestive enzymes.

3. The third, or breath, chakra is linked to the adrenal glands, secretors of adrenaline and other hormones in response to stress.

4. The fourth chakra, the heart chakra, is in the location of the thymus, an organ of the immune system.

5. The fifth chakra, the throat chakra, is associated with the thyroid gland, which controls metabolism, makes proteins and controls how sensitive the body is to other hormones.

6. The sixth chakra, the brow chakra, is located with the pituitary gland, which releases brain chemicals that promote proper growth of glands and organs.

7. The seventh chakra is associated with the pineal gland, which secretes a variety of hormones. It is light sensitive and affects circadian rhythms.

Ductless gland secretions regulate all body functions. This can't be overstated. The endocrine system coordinates the functions of the various organs and cells and determines the body's weight and overall health. The endocrine system in turn depends upon healthy chakra function for proper flow of life force energy.

NADI AGAIN

The main nadi that runs the length of the spinal column to the crown of the head through the chakras is named the Sushumna in the Sanskrit tradition. Two other major nadis run along side the Sushumna and are normally the main conduits of prana. Although the Sushumna has the greatest carrying capacity, it habitually lies dormant and these large secondary channels carry the pranic energy.

Both secondary channels start at the first chakra (the Ida on the left side and the Pingala on the right) and ascend the spinal column. They pierce each chakra in turn, changing sides of the spine at each chakra, forming a double helix pattern, until terminating at the sixth, or third eye, chakra. The Ida originates and terminates on the left side and is considered part of the left nadi system. The Pingala starts and ends on the right side of the Sushumna and is part of the right nadi system.

During the course of a normal day, we breathe using both nostrils only for ten breaths each hour. For the majority of time either the right or left nostril dominates. For an hour at sunrise and an hour at dusk both nostrils are utilized evenly. Although this isn't common knowledge, it can be confirmed by observation.

When the left nostril is dominant, the Ida is most active and the left side of the brain is more stimulated. When the right nostril is dominant, the Pingala is most utilized and the majority of stimulation is to the right hemisphere. When both nostrils are used evenly, both sides of the brain are stimulated.

Being aware of this relationship, yogis consider early morning or early evening the most effective times to meditate. This is why we do Alternate Nostril Breathing before meditation. Alternate Nostril Breathing causes the Ida and Pingala to come back into balance and provides pranic energy to both brain hemispheres. Being aware of which nostril is dominant can help us be more efficient in our affairs, doing right brain activities when the Pingala is the main conduit of life force and left-brain activities when the Ida is dominant.

As you know, the brain has increased in size with our evolution. The lower brain at the top of the spinal cord is the oldest portion and controls basic animal functions. Growing on top of that is the mammal brain. It controls more complex brain functions. On top of that is the cerebral cortex, which provides our higher intelligence whose full potential is yet to be completely utilized.

The lower brain stem is associated with the first three chakras as expressed through basic instincts, and the midbrain is associated with sentimentality and the emotions – fourth, fifth, and sixth chakra qualities. Creative thinking and inspiration are the purview of the cerebral cortex, attributes of the sixth and seventh chakras. Between the two hemispheres, at the crown of the head, is the portal to supreme consciousness.

The Ida and Pingala crisscross from the first to the sixth chakra, ending behind the eyes. They don't fully nurture the highest centers of the brain. The Sushumna terminates at the cerebral cortex. The energy coming through it flows over the cerebral cortex and enriches the highest brain functions. This is an object of meditation, to clear the dormant Sushumna, allowing unrestricted pranic energy to flood the brain.

APANA

In the lower core of the body, between the anus and the navel, a unique form of pranic energy, 'apana' in Sanskrit, is found. It is concerned with the assimilation of food, waste removal, and sexual function. Apana is also the energy that pushes us out of the womb during birth and is often referred to as pelvic prana. Apana is involved with material existence, but carries the latent potential to transform into spiritual energy.

When we focus our attention on an area of the body, we energize the object of our attention. Energy follows attention.

CHAKRA FOCUS

The chakras are energy centers along the spinal column. When focusing on the chakras, the meditator need not be mentally concerned with exact location. A feel for location develops with practice. The best tool for exploring the chakras is relaxation. Just go to that general place, let go, and simply be. It depends less on 'doing' than 'knowing', less on 'knowing' than 'feeling', and less on 'feeling' than 'being'. It can't be overstated–relax.

The chakras are unique and need to be directly observed by each individual meditator. They may be experienced differently at different times and many descriptions of their nature have resulted. A popular view from the Hindu tradition is that each resembles a lotus flower, with different chakras composed of varying numbers of petals. Each energy center might appear as a world or reality unto itself with its own rules and setting. Observing the function of the chakras, they can each be seen as a vortex of energy, like a cyclone. The vortex of the first chakra spins clockwise, the second, counterclockwise, and the third, clockwise. The direction of spin alternates as the spine is ascended. As the meditator becomes more at home within their chakra awareness, they notice qualities inherent to the direction of spin. The clockwise spinning chakras are dynamic in the sense they tend to project out into reality, like the sexual nature of the first chakra, the expulsion of breath of the third chakra, speaking at the fifth chakra and so on. For this reason, they are often thought of as having more masculine traits. The counterclockwise spinning chakras are more receiving, like the nourishment received from the mother through the umbilical cord at the navel chakra, the love received through the heart chakra, and the stimulus received by the third eye. These chakras are thought of as being more feminine in nature.

Our meditation starts with focusing on the perineum, the part of the body between the legs, from the anus to one's sex. This has a stimulating effect and can be very pleasurable. It is the beginning of the arousal of apana. The meditator is asked to envision, seeing with the minds eye, or third eye, the area as a deep dark brown, almost black, like rich fertile top soil. With our focus on the perineum, we are being grounded. Feel through the bottoms of the legs and buttocks to the ground below.

The meditator is being grounded to the earth, one of the five material elements that combine to structure reality on the physical plane: earth, water, fire, air, and space. Grounding links one with the core of the mother planet, Earth. This grounding is everything that supports the meditator, and all that composes him or her at this precise moment in time. Past incarnations, family and cultural history, genetic makeup, environment, and life experience are all realized in this point of focus. This isn't a thought process. It just is.

The energy of attention stimulates latent apana. Because of the sexual nature of the pelvic prana, sensual arousal might occur. Just observe and accept. There is no need to censure the experience. Enjoy the meditation in observer consciousness.

After a set number of breaths, the attention moves up to the first chakra. If the meditator has time, he or she can relax into the experience and allow the attention to percolate up to the sacrum on its own. The first chakra is awash with the color red. When initially meditating, all the aspirant needs to be aware of is the color expressed through each chakra. With practice, all that will be necessary is to touch the front of the body over a particular chakra and the color associated with it will appear before the mind's eye. Relax into the hue, feel it as much as visualize it. The shade of the color may vary from meditation to meditation and can be an indicator of the influences the person is presently under.

Each chakra can be thought of as entering another room. After the aspirant gets comfortable in these different rooms, she or he will relax more deeply and notice different characteristics inherent to each.

FIRST CHAKRA

The first chakra is a beautiful bright red and is representative of the element earth. The first time meditator may feel fear. The first chakra is associated with the birth process and entering the world for the first time. Everything is new. This experience mirrors the aspirant's entrance into meditation. Both are natural processes and promise wonder and growth.

This is the part of the body housing the organs of digestion and elimination. The sacrum center is primordial. It has to do with our most animal nature, sexual passion, which brings forth human form to clothe another soul. As the most inherently physical of the chakras its realm is that most physical of pleasures, sexual ecstasy.

SECOND CHAKRA

The second chakra is a vibrant orange and its element is water. Its location is the center of the physical body. The navel is what remains from the umbilical cord that nourished our development in the womb where we are dependent on our host mother for life. Apana energized the erection and fueled the passion, propelled the egg to the fallopian tubes and the sperm to their union. Apana was the life force for the dividing zygote until nadis developed with the development of the umbilical connection to the prana of the mother's body. As the embryo grew and became more complex, no longer was absorption of the mother's apana adequate for further growth. Prana from the mother, through the umbilical, gradually replaced it as a source of life force. The mother's apana provides energy for the birth contractions, forcing the child into the world.

The newborn enters the world separate from the mother. It exhales, and then inhales a first breath. Breathing begins with an exhalation and the last breath at death is an inhalation. With that first breath cycle, the new being draws life force into the body as an individual for the first time. This is the moment of the beginning of life. The spirit enters the body. Before, the now sentient being, was a complex growth within the mother's body. At the moment of life, with that first breath cycle, the circulation of blood in the infant's body reverses direction. The heart pumps in the opposite direction and the blood that was being pushed though the veins out though the circulatory system is pushed though the arteries and returns to the heart through the veins. A soul has entered the little body, having picked the perfect set of parents, in the perfect set of circumstances, to give it an opportunity to experience what's necessary for this cycle of spiritual growth. Free will determines how well the opportunity is utilized.

THIRD CHAKRA

The color of the third chakra is bright yellow and its element is fire. The third chakra is the meeting place of the apana of the lower core of the body and the prana of the upper body. The first and second chakra are negatively charged with apana, and the fourth and fifth chakra are positively charged with prana–a living battery. As the meditator focuses awareness on the third chakra and the apana moves up the Sushumna to the area of the diaphragm, the negative ions of apana mix with the positive ions of the prana. This causes a fusion reaction similar to what occurs in the sun. The third chakra can be envisioned as the sun. Just as the sun provides the energy for life on our physical world, energy from the third chakra radiates down, stirring and reinvigorating the apana below, which can otherwise become stagnant. This new combined energy also shines upward illuminating our subtler inner spiritual world.

FOURTH CHAKRA

The fourth, or heart chakra's, color is a beautiful chlorophyll green and its element is air. The lower three chakras are the material universe and the fourth chakra is the transition point to our divine spiritual manifestation. The heart chakra is the point of transition and the upper three chakras are the higher, or spiritual, centers. The ascending line of energy through the Sushumna parallels the evolutionary ascent of humankind from animal to spiritual being. A horizontal line, the point of transition, forms a cross. This is the symbol of the fourth chakra. The teachings of Jesus are fourth chakra teachings. "…And now these three remain: faith, hope and love. But the greatest of these is love." The Beatles' *All You Need is Love* is also an expression of fourth chakra teaching. Astrology, based on observations of earth in relationship to its slowly changing stellar influences, divided earthly time into two thousand year segments, or ages. We are now leaving the segment when the teachings of Jesus were to manifest as the prevailing order. This era, the Piscean Age, shares with Jesus the symbol of the fish. The new age we're starting to enter is the Aquarian Age, the age of understanding. If we can get our tails over the fence, we will begin to share the promise of the miracles Jesus taught are our birthright.

FIFTH CHAKRA

The fifth chakra's color is light blue, like a clear light blue sky. The element associated with the throat chakra is space. Understanding and learning are two of its qualities. Rather than accumulation of knowledge (what there is to know is infinite and always changing), what is needed is an understanding of the eternal and how to be a part of that constant. Space is by far the largest component of the material world. Look up at the night sky and see the vast distances between the stars. The distance between the individual atomic particles that make us up are proportionally as great. We, and everything in the physical universe, are comprised of very little actual matter. The energy that binds that matter forms the impression of things being solid.

SIXTH CHAKRA

The color of the third eye chakra is a deep dark blue, like the sky on a moonless night. The sixth chakra is not associated with an element because self-realization places us beyond the material universe. The third eye is the seat of awareness. Another name for the third eye is the mind's eye. It is utilized to form all visualizations. Its location places it with the pituitary gland. Medical science can measure increased production of beneficial brain chemicals such as endorphins, melatonin, and serotonin when attention is focused on the third eye during meditation.

In Sanskrit, the yogis lumped all the pleasurable brain chemicals together calling them 'Amrita'. A mudra is performed, curling the tongue to the back of the roof of the mouth as if to taste the Amrita. This helps to stimulate its production and is called the Shiva Mudra.

Awareness of eternal knowledge comes when all desires move up to the sixth chakra. All the body elements are balanced and being is centered in blissful non-duality and the realization of oneness. The elements are present in their pure essence, fostering self-realization.

SEVENTH CHAKRA

Awareness floats up to the crown chakra. A yarmulke of ultra-violet is over the skull. Here the illusion of the individual self is dissolved. One is their own real true self, at one with the cosmic principles within the body that govern the entire universe. This is the essence of being, a reflection of the cosmic absolute where it is possible to realize the divine.

With grace, awareness floats above the head into the super conscious, the domain of existence beyond our physical plane. Being is now released from familiar foregone dimensions. Being, the quintessence of infinity, shimmers, a thousand-petal lotus with a radiance of such a pure white that all the colors of the spectrum glisten within its brilliance.

INTEGRATE ALL THE CHAKRAS

Swing the arms overhead in a wide arc.

Bring the hands together, capturing this divine energy in the palms.

Lower the hands in prayer mudra to the top of the head, with elbows extended wide.

Pause and bask in the ultra-violet mixing with the brilliant white drawn down from above.

Lower the palms touching the forehead in front of the third eye, bringing the elbows together.

Feel the deep blue of the brow center mixing with the light from the higher center.

Lower the prayer position hands down over the throat center, open the elbows again and pause and feel the light blue light mix with the colors from above.

Bring the hands down over the heart with the elbows down at your sides.

Feel the cosmic energy mix with the deep green of the heart center.

With the hands still in prayer mudra over the heart, see the yellow of the diaphragm or breath center, then see the orange of the navel center, down to the red of the sacrum center and see down to the deep rich brown of the perineum and on below.

Feel the energy extend forty feet below you and rise up forty feet above your head with your heart glowing at the center. See if you can feel the energy undulating in waves the length of your being.

Bring awareness back to your heart. From here, the heart, you face the world. Feel love.

Lift the palms again to the brow center, elbows together, and utter, "The divine in me recognizes the divine in you and All".

Place the hands back over the heart and say, "Namaste," aloud.

Bending at the waist and extending the arms, bow forward.

FINE TUNING

VIBRATION

Everything is vibration. When you chant "OM," your voice resonates across the universe like the ripples created when a stone is dropped into a pond. This goes on forever.

Each octave of vibration (comparable to do re mi fa so la ti do) flows out of a preceding octave and into the following one: each octave (including both the 'do' notes) has half the frequency of the octave above it, and twice the frequency of the octave below it. This too is a continuum, stretching beyond the limits of hearing and finally beyond the limits of measure. All is a progression along infinite scales. Frequency determines the mode of existence – the manifestation of all phenomena.

The fundamental sound is OM.

Because nature repeats its successful solutions, if we can understand one of those matrixes within our range of perception, we can extend that understanding to natural constructions beyond our perceptual limitations. Sound lends itself to an understanding of vibration. Sound waves are slow enough we can feel, measure and sometimes even see them. Music is an expression of our delight with this ability.

Do, Re, Mi, (half step and a curve) Fa, So, La, (half step and a curve) Ti, Do. The musical major scale as an octave demonstrates the vibrational pattern taken by all forms of energy. With each half step reality curves, as can be seen on a grand scale through astronomical observation. The universe is a curved universe.

Everything is vibration and is expressed in waves of varying frequencies, from the smallest theoretical sub-particles to galaxies. Everything is one cosmic composition, creation's symphony of coalescence. Every part of a person is vibrating and, ideally, those melodious vibrations can combine to harmonize with creation.

Each chakra has a tone that can be heard in deep meditation. LANG is the sound of the first chakra. VANG is the sound of the second chakra. DANG is the sound of the third chakra. YANG is the sound of the forth chakra. HANG is the sound of the fifth chakra. AUM is the sound of the sixth chakra. The sound for the seventh chakra is OM, sounding continuously with no break. OM as the subtle undertone of the breath resonating the content of each inhale, exhale, and pause; OM, the continuum.

While meditating on the chakras, at each chakra its sound (vibration) can be chanted, increasing energy.

To enhance an activity associated with a specific chakra, that chakra's sound can be chanted. As an example, LANG increases sexual energy or can aid with childbirth.

THE FUNDAMENTAL SOUND IS OM.

One of the oldest mantras (chants) that has been passed down verbally since the dawn of humanity, (in Sanskrit) is the Sri Gayathri:

> OM bhur bhuvah suvah,
>
> Tatsavitur varenyam,
>
> Bhargo devasya dhimahi,
>
> Dhiyoyonah prachodayat,
>
> OM apo jyotiraso amrtam brahma,
>
> Bhur bhuvah suvarom.

An English translation:

> Om (pervades) earth, atmosphere, and heavens.
>
> That self luminous, brilliant Divinity, who is Supreme Source,
>
> On that we meditate.
>
> May the sacred light illuminate our perceptions.
>
> Om is the waters, the light essence, immortal reality,
>
> Pervading earth, atmosphere, and heavens.

Om is the prime vibration, encompassing 'All'. Many chants are utilized to gain higher spiritual states. Some have specific functions, lesser goals, but 'Oneness' is best achieved and expressed through 'OM'. This is vocalized by making the 'Ah' sound, the 'Um' sound, and the 'Oh mmm' sound at the same time. The sound starts at the very back of the throat and slowly progresses forward though the mouth and ends with the vibration of the lips. Doing this you make all the vowel sounds.

The 'OM' sound has five parts, the Ah, the Oh, the Um, the stillness of the mouth, throat and lips, and the vibration of the mouth, throat and lips.

Anyone who has chanted in a group can attest to the power of that experience. The sound energy can be felt on the skin and seen with the eyes. Truly, it is a case where the whole is greater than the sum of its parts.

This concept that everything is vibration is reflected in the Old Testament:

In the beginning was the Word.

KOSHAS

All spiritual traditions assume that the physical body isn't the only vehicle in which consciousness can express itself or in which the Self or Spirit manifests itself. In yoga, five sheaths (the five koshas) are recognized as occluding the pure light of the transcendental Self.

Yoga reveals the consciousness of the individual as a partial expression of cosmic consciousness. The ultimate reality producing mind and matter is consciousness. From minerals to human form, consciousness exists on an extensive spectrum of many levels.

Individual consciousness and cosmic consciousness are one, separated by subjectivity. Humans have evolved to be capable of understanding beyond sensory perception for spiritual growth.

Consciousness is purusa, unchanging. In order to exist as a material life form it must combine with matter that is always changing, prakriti. This is a paradox. The Hindu yogic tradition uses the myth of Shiva and Shakti to explain.

They are a divine couple, lovers in the field of creation. Shiva is the seer, purusa, never changing, and Shakti is energy, prakriti, always changing. Shakti, the lover, wants to play a game of passion and creates a world inviting Shiva, the beloved, in to join her. Shiva points out the world is always changing and he is always the same. How can he play in her creation?

"You be the center," she replies. "You remain in your unchanging bliss and I'll intermediate between you and the outside world. I will build sheaths through which you can experience the fun of my world while doing nothing in eternal bliss."

Five koshas surround Shiva, allowing the lovers to experience passion as the embodied soul.

1. The Self in the Sheath of Bliss (in Sanskrit, the Anandamaya Kosha), surrounds the absolute self. Absolute truth, a point, is never changing. It and the bliss are forever and always protected on all sides. The Self is the truth, and truth is never changing. Everything else is always in a state of flux, always changing. The Self realizes all else is illusion. The Self can be compared to a movie screen. While the film is playing, all sorts of action is going on, but when the movie is finished, the screen is exactly like it was before, untouched by what appeared to be taking place. Bliss just is. It is not of the mind, but the peace, love and joy that is this level of reality. Even this can be released to be pure self, in Sanskrit, 'Atman'. The Anandamaya Kosha is still a sheath covering the Atman. It's as if the true self is a

light and the kosha a lampshade covering it. Even though the Anandamaya Kosha is the subtlest of koshas, it still suppresses the full magnitude of the light. One is reminded of the Biblical admonishment to take your light from beneath the bushel basket.

2. The next sheath is the sheath of knowing (the Vijnanamaya Kosha). This knowing is beyond the information of the senses. This is the paradox of seeing what is in the illusion. The ego (intellect) forms structure from experience, but at some point perceives the structure as only that, a construct. Here is understanding on the highest level, unfiltered intuition. Here we have the deepest insights, as we experience the moment. Sometimes called the 'wisdom body', the Vijnanamaya Kosha is insight, integration and wholeness.

3. Next is the sheath of the mind (the Manomaya Kosha). Often called the mental body, it is the tool consciousness uses to perceive the world. The mind uses the brain as a tool to process information and performs at every level of the body. It utilizes the sense organs to gather stimulus and the mind stores and sorts information drawing conclusions. The intellect's sense of self, the 'I' that is the ego (composed of memory, everything you've been taught about the world and about yourself) is also within this sheath. The Manomaya Kosha is also the seat of the emotions. The Manomaya Kosha must be tamed to allow you to be at home in the more subtle koshas.

4. The sheath of energy or life force is next (the Pranamaya Kosha). It supplies energy to all components of the body and keeps it alive. The air element, or pranic force, creates vibration and life. Prana rides the breath. It allows our true self to animate in the physical universe. It initiates life. The Old Testament tells of God breathing life into Adam.

5. The outermost of the koshas is the physical body (the Annamaya Kosha). 'Anna', in Sanskrit means food, and this is the body formed by the ingestion of food. It is sometimes referred to as the 'gross body', the least subtle of the koshas. The physical body is the temple of the soul. It houses organs that make it possible for consciousness to exist on this physical plane. It deserves care and respect. The reasons for being on the physical plane are the lessons that can only be learned in this material form. If the physical body is not properly maintained, it can be more difficult to advance spiritually. Another paradox: the Annamaya Kosha is the most gross and dense of the koshas, but it is the most malleable. It is actually a manifestation of the unseen, more subtle koshas, and a balanced sincere effort

toward spiritual awareness echoes throughout the body and is reflected in the physical form.

Familiarity with the koshas suggests similarity with a hologram, a three dimensional photographic image made with laser technology. The light of the laser shines through a crystal and produces a refracted effigy of the object portrayed therein. The light of the spirit shines through the koshas projecting the individual human being.

THE EIGHT LIMBS

After thousands of years of individuals practicing yoga under the direction of a teacher or guru who would orally pass down the traditions that guru had learned from their own teacher, a basic path was put into writing. Around 200 AD the text, the Yoga Sutra, appeared. It is attributed to Patanjali, although it might have arisen through a group effort. Little is known of its origins. Some consider it a response to the growing popularity of Buddhism to remind spiritual seekers of the reach of yoga beyond what they perceived as the goals of Buddhist teachings.

The Yoga Sutra describes a basic system for the practice of yoga, an eight- limbed path for fostering connection to the divine. The 'Eight Limbs' are a blueprint of a holistic practice fostering peace, health, and understanding to create balance and unity with the whole of creation. Although practiced for thousands of years, the steps to yoga were now codified.

All of the eight limbs are of equal importance, but are presented in an order, that for most individuals, present a systematic approach.

1. Yama: Universal morality

2. Niyama: Personal observances

3. Asana: Body Postures

4. Pranayama: Control of prana through breathing exercises

5. Pratyahara: Withdrawal from the senses

6. Dharana: Inner awareness and concentration

7. Dhyana: Devotion and meditation on the divine

8. Samadi: Divine union

Practice of the Eight Limbs will balance the individual, creating the mental and physical health necessary for an exploration leading to an understanding of the inner self. It is a road map. The journey and discoveries are distinctive to each person. The Eight Limbs are observances that allow individuals to explore their unique personal path to realize their full potential.

The first two steps are concerned with ethics–our actions and attitudes towards our self and others. Yama is our feelings and actions toward things and persons around us, a universal morality. Niyama is our inner relationship with our self. Both direct our energy positively, fostering a human nature benevolent to self and our surroundings.

I. UNIVERSAL MORALITY, THE YAMAS

1. Ahimsa, Compassion: Ahimsa is not harming any living thing, practicing nonviolence in the form of kindness and consideration and a lack of cruelty while being responsible for the well being of all.

2. Satya, Truthfulness: Satya translates 'speaking truth'. Honesty is the best policy, but because Ahimsa is listed first, at times it might be better to be silent. Truth is the foundation of trust.

3. Asteya, Non-stealing: Asteya means not taking anything that isn't freely given. This includes maintaining confidences and having pure intentions as well as respecting others' material possessions.

4. Brachmacharya, Responsible Use of Sexual Energy: Brachmacharya implies sexual energy should be employed to further our higher spiritual aspirations. Sometimes this may mean celibacy, but sexual energy and sensuality are also considered powerful assets to be enjoyed responsibly in the quest for wholeness.

5. Aparigraha, Without Greed: Aparigraha is letting go of attachments and welcoming change with the assurance things will work out for the best. Greed and hoarding display a lack of understanding that our needs will be met through an unfolding of the future that is beyond our ability to predict. Having just enough is sharing with others and maintains a balanced environment.

Observance of the positive behavior described through the yamas is practiced as a way of life and will purify the individual, create a joyful, sustainable world for them to inhabit, and prevent and remove outside obstacles to fulfillment.

II. THE PERSONAL OBSERVANCES, NIYAMA

Criteria for life, the niyamas are a personal set of rules for the way we perceive our intimate self.

1. Purity, Sauca: Sauca is purity on the physical and mental levels–cleanliness of the outer body as well as the inner body. Asana removes toxins from the body and pranayama oxygenates the blood and purifies the nervous system. The mind should be clean of negative emotions and thoughts.

2. Contentment, Santosa: Everything has a purpose, karma. Accept your lot in life and be grateful for what you have instead of dwelling on your desires. Be content. Realize life's difficulties are opportunities for learning. Be at peace with your situation.

3. Devotion, Tapas: Tapas literally means 'heat'. The heat of devotion burns away obstructions to our spiritual advancement. Being enthusiastic in all we do allows our energy to be most effectively directed towards realization of our full spiritual potential.

4. Self-awareness, Svadhyaya: Maintain self-reflective attention to all activities. Be aware of what is being done and how activities are accomplished. Be centered in observer consciousness and make a study of one's self. Examine yourself and remember, "Physician heal yourself."

5. Rejoice in the divine, Isvarapranidhana: Be aware of the divine in your fellows and all. Namaste. Sing praises to the Lord. Everything is part of a sacrosanct unfolding–wonder at the grand design and savor your role in its manifestation. Attune yourself to the universal consciousness so that you may assume your role as a part of the creator and live life as a fully spiritual being.

III. BODY POSTURES, ASANAS

Moving into and holding various configurations of the physical body as part of the practice of yoga is called asana. When people in the West think of yoga, this narrow range of the total discipline commonly comes to mind. In Sanskrit, 'asana' translates as 'seat' or 'seat next to the teacher', expressing the need to be comfortable in the body before other learning can commence. Asana practice improves health, strength, flexibility and balance. The lymphatic system of the body needs movement and the flexing of muscles to propel lymph fluids through the body. All the components of the body need to be exercised to maintain optimum function. Without stimulation they tend to atrophy.

Asana helps to calm the mind and temper emotions. Challenging the physical body helps the practitioner connect with the other levels of self. Because of the rapid ability of the physical body to reflect change, it demonstrates the capacity to change on deeper unseen levels. The physical body is our home in this reality. Memories can be stored in our tissues. Asana is a way of strengthening the will and exploring our psychological makeup, creating a balance between our material and spiritual existence.

Because asana quiets the mind, it is a preparation for meditation. Indeed, it can be a form of meditation. It fosters awareness of the mind's functioning, the body's state of wellbeing, and the mechanics of breath. Asana helps us reconnect with the vast wisdom that controls and directs body function, the same wisdom that wants to bring our body into healthy balance.

IV. BREATH CONTROL, PRANAYAMA

Pranayama is used to control, direct, and measure breath through various techniques. Because prana, the life force energy, rides the breath, pranayama has remarkable powers of transformation.

Many body functions are directed by the autonomic nervous system and operate without our control. Other physical actions are consciously directed by our thoughts and intentions. Breath is the one function that is in between, straddling both the automatic and conscious systems. The body breathes perfectly well without any conscious direction, but we can also intervene and control our breathing. This gives us the potential to influence the life force energy within our bodies.

The Yoga Sutras consider pranayama, along with asana, to be the most effective means of purifying the body and mind. Both produce heat (tapas) the inner fire of purification. The subtle energy channels of the body, the nadis, are cleansed of obstructions to the vital force. This promotes healthy balance within the body and stimulates the higher centers of consciousness. Pranayama soothes and calms the mind. This reduces cravings.

V. WITHDRAWAL FROM THE SENSES, PRATYAHARA

'Pratya' is withdrawal in Sanskrit, while 'ahara' means nourishment. Pratyahara helps us detach from sensory distractions that pull us away from our spiritual intentions. The senses are no longer fed a diet of external stimulation, allowing for the internal peace of self-realization.

The senses are no longer permitted to dominate the mind. Energy isn't flowing out to each distraction and the senses withdraw. With meditation, the focus of meditation absorbs the awareness, producing sensory restraint. The senses follow the object of awareness instead of distracting one's attention. Because the mind is so focused, the senses follow the mind.

When the senses don't chase after stimulation, they concentrate full attention on the limited stimulus they are permitted. Sense perception becomes keener. Because the range of attention is narrower, it is sharper.

When the senses are no longer in control, cravings diminish. We no longer eat because we have a craving, attempting to placate sensory arousal. We eat because we need to eat.

Yoga teaches us to observe our own mind. We become aware of the influence of outside stimulus and how it prevents tranquility and introspection. We overcome the imbalance that is created by our efforts to enhance some sensations and avoid others. This judgment is a waste of energy that could be better used by watching the operation of our mind to move toward enlightenment.

VI. INNER AWARENESS AND CONCENTRATION, DHARANA

When the mind has been purified through the practice of yoga, it is able to focus. Asana makes us comfortable in our own skin. The tapas of pranayama cleanses the mind and pratyahara tempers the senses so we can become single-mindedly engrossed. The mind no longer thinks about events in the past or future, but is fully in the moment. We are the activity at hand and not a reverie. Concentration brings us to full alertness. The mind, intellect, and ego are all restrained and we are intensely awake.

VII. DEVOTION AND MEDITATION ON THE DIVINE, DHYANA

Dhyana is concentration on the Divine so intentional, so devoted, the meditator becomes the object of intention. The meditator merges with the Divine. Everything else is set aside, is out of the consciousness, no longer exists in the consciousness. The focus of concentration on oneness can be so singular, the mind is transformed into oneness.

Reflecting on truth, the Absolute, we perceive reality beyond illusion. We differentiate between the perceiver and the perceived. The observer isn't the object of observation. The object of observation is transitory, illusory. The observer just 'is' as in the Biblical admonition of the Divine, "I am that I am".

VIII. DIVINE UNION, SAMADHI

Samadhi translates to 'coalesce', or merge. This is a state of pure awareness of pure identity. The senses are completely put behind. The conscious mind merges with the super-consciousness from which it emerged. Samadhi is complete union. Individual and totality, object and field are no longer separated. This is true Yoga, the yoking, or absorbing of the profane by the Divine, complete union.

With the attainment of Samadhi there is no longer the illusion of 'I'. Self is no longer distinguished from non-self. The mind and intellect are at complete rest and there is only consciousness, from which everything originally arose.

COMPLETE TEN-MINUTE YOGA WORKOUT

Now that you've gained a degree of comfort performing the Morning Ritual, it is beneficial and fun to learn more asana. The Workout is forty-eight postures organized in a flowing sequence. The arrangement allows for efficient movement so a lot can be done in a short time. Once it is familiar, the entire routine can be performed in ten minutes, not counting the time you choose to relax in Seated Meditation or in Corpse Posture at the finish. As with learning any posture, at first do the best you can, even if you feel you're just going through the motions. You will be surprised how quickly the body will learn the new movements. Even though the practice encourages you to relax, existence in the modern world makes many demands upon your time. Yoga is one of the most important activities in your schedule. The practice can be condensed so every part of the body is stretched and made limber while consuming a minimal amount of time.

To begin, stand with feet slightly apart and firmly planted on the floor. [Photo 30] Stand straight, but relaxed, with palms slightly revolved forward and shoulders at ease. Gently extend through the crown of the head and soften the focus of the eyes.

Let go of extraneous thoughts and be aware of your breath.

Rock forward on the feet and come up as high as possible on the toes. [Photo 31]

Rock back on the feet. Put the weight on the heels and lift the front of the feet off the ground. [Photo 32]

Lift the inside edges of both feet, placing the weight on the outside edges. Press toes in and make exaggerated arches. [Photo 33]

Repeat all three above foot actions, four times.

With feet flat on the floor, lift your big toes while keeping the other toes on the ground. [Photo 34]

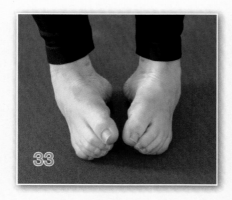

Hold the big toes down and lift the all the other toes. [Photo 35]

Do both sides four times. These are actions most of us have never done before. With a little practice, they can be a good example of how quickly the body learns.

36

Lift your right leg so the thigh is parallel to the ground with the leg bent and the lower leg hanging at a right angle. With the leg held in this position, rotate the foot at the ankle, clockwise four times, and then counter-clockwise four times. [Photo 36]

Repeat the same motions on the left side.

37

Standing upright, bend deeply at the knees. While holding the rest of the body still, rotate both knees in big circles to the right four times, and then big circles to the left four times. [Photo 37]

Straighten legs and stand completely upright with both arms fully extended. Twisting at the waist, spin the upper half of the body all the way to the right. Pause, and then rotate the upper half of the body, spinning fully to the left. [Photo 38]

Repeat four times.

Return to center and extend forward from the waist. Relax into a forward bend. [Photo 39] For additional stretch, grab each elbow with the opposite hand and straighten the legs.

Extend both arms low behind the back and interlock the hands. [Photo 40]

Pull back on the hands drawing the shoulder blades together.

Release your grip and start lifting the arms slowly while keeping the shoulder blades close together. [Photo 41]

When palms come together overhead, look up at the hands and rise up on to the toes. [Photo 42]

At first you may have to stand flat-footed. Return your gaze forward as you lower the heels while lowering the arms to the starting position. Keep the shoulder blades close together. Repeat four times.

Standing, raise both arms above the head and turn the hands so the back of the hands are together behind the head. Pull both hands down between the shoulder blades while pressing the elbows back. [Photo 43]

Hold this position a few moments, feeling the stretch.

Still holding the position with the arms, turn the right foot to the left, placing the toes against the arch of the left foot. Rotate the body to the right. [Photo 44]

Reverse the position of the feet, left toes in the right arch, and twist the body to the left. Perform this one time in each direction.

Standing with feet apart, reach the right arm into the air and then let it fold back at the elbow so the fingers rest on the upper back of the right shoulder blade. Bend the left arm up behind the back, reaching for the right shoulder blade. [Photo 45]

Pull both hands towards each other and, if you are flexible enough, interlock the fingers of the two hands.

Do the reverse on the opposite side then gently release your arms.

Standing with arms relaxed at your sides, roll the head to the right, then to the back, from the back to the left, and then from the left to forward. [Photo 46]

After several rotations in that direction, reverse and rotate the head in the opposite direction several times.

Standing with feet slightly apart, raise the arms overhead and grab the left wrist with the right hand. Pushing the hips to the left, pull the left wrist to the right, creating a half moon shape with the body. [Photo 47]

Do the opposite, creating a half moon shape the other way. Do this one time on each side.

Standing with feet together, extend the arms overhead, palms together. Keeping the lower body rigid, bend forward at the waist keeping a straight back and the arms straight out from the shoulders. Bending only at the waist, bend forward until you touch the floor - if possible. [Photo 48]

Still keeping the back straight and bending the knees slightly if necessary, slowly rise, only flexing at the waist. Do this once.

Lie on the back with arms on the floor, straight out from the shoulders, perpendicular to the torso. With knees pointing up, feet hip width apart, draw the heels toward the buttocks, soles on the ground. Let the knees fall to the

right, keeping the left shoulder touching the ground, and turning the head to the left. [Photo 49]

Reverse the movements, letting the knees fall to the left. Go back and forth, two times each side.

Staying in the same position on the back, extend the legs together, straight up. Allow the straight legs to fall as far as comfortably possible to the right. [Photo 50] Feet go all the way to the floor if you are flexible

enough, while turning the head to the left and keeping the left shoulder on the ground.

Perform the same actions on the other side. Do both sides two times. On the back, with arms extended straight out from the shoulders and palms

on the floor, lift the knees so the calves are parallel to the floor. Extend the feet away from the body and make a circle to the right and back to center with the calves parallel to the floor. [Photo 51]

Repeat, swinging the legs in a circle to the right a second time. Do the opposite twice, swinging the legs to the left in a wide circle.

Come to a seated position, with the legs extended straight in front. Place each hand below its corresponding knee and bend the knees, feet on the floor. Lift the legs so the calves are parallel to the floor, balancing on the tailbone. [Photo 52]

Slowly count to 8.

Lie on the back with arms by the sides, palms down. Pressing on the palms, swing the legs overhead, past center and as close to the floor above your head as possible. [Photo 53]

Hold to a slow count of four.

54

Place hands under the hips and raise both legs perpendicular to the floor. [Photo 54]

Hold for a slow count of four.

Roll down, palms under knees.

Keeping the knees bent, rock up on the spine so the feet almost touch the floor. Rock back on the spine. Bring the feet as close to the floor as comfortable above the head. [Photo 55]

Rock back and forth on the length of the spine four times.

55

At the top of the fourth rock, grab the big toe of each foot with the first two fingers of the corresponding hand. Extend the legs in a wide 'V' and balance on the tailbone. [Photo 56]

Rest here for a slow count of four.

Roll on to the stomach, palms on the floor under the shoulders. Press the tops of the feet into the floor. Draw in the belly, anchor the pelvis to the floor and lift the upper half of the body. [Photo 57]

If possible, lift the hands from the floor and hold for a slow count of four.

Place the palms on the floor below the shoulders. While keeping the elbows close to the body, lift the upper half of the body, using both the back muscles and the arms. [Photo 58] Lift the upper torso as high as possible. Keep the thighs anchored to the ground. Hold for a slow count of four.

Straighten the arms so the weight is on the palms and the tops of the feet. [Photo 59] Look up and let the spine relax. Hold for a slow count of four.

Sit on the backs of the thighs and relax forward at the waist. Extend the arms on the floor in front of you. [Photo 60]

Relax the upper body onto the tops of the thighs and stretch the arms forward for a count of four.

With the feet together, spread the knees wide and relax the body close to the floor. Relax the bent arms with the hands close to the head. [Photo 61]

Relax into the posture for a moment.

Draw the knees closer together and relax with the hands resting alongside the legs. [Photo 62]

Forehead rests on the floor as you pause.

Rise up onto the hands and knees. Extend the right arm and the left leg and hover. [Photo 63]

Put that arm and leg down and extend the left arm and the right leg and hover.

Return to hands and knees and exhale.

Push the buttocks forward and arch the spine and draw in the belly. [Photo 64]

Pause.

Inhale and lower the spine in the opposite direction, with belly down and head up. [Photo 65]

Pause.

Turn toes under, straighten your legs and push back and up through the tailbone. Relax the head and shoulders and press down with the hands. Fingers are wide and the stomach is drawn in. [Photo 66] Push your heels toward the ground.

Pause.

Come to a seated position, legs extended straight to the front. Relax and bend at the waist, folding on to the body with the arms extended forward. [Photo 67]

Pause.

Sitting up with legs straight in front of you, place the palms down and extend through the crown of the head and the soles of the feet. [Photo 68]

Sit up straight.

Pause and stretch.

Grab the big toes with the first two fingers of the corresponding hand. Pull forward, bending at the waist, while holding the head high and arching the back and shoulders. [Photo 69]

Pull the stomach in and pause.

Sit up straight with legs together and extended.
Place the left hand on the right knee and the right hand on the floor just behind the tailbone. Use the leverage of the left hand to twist the torso above the waist to the right while looking that direction with a turned head. [Photo 70]

Do the reverse to the other side.

Spread open your straight legs as wide as possible, and bend forward at the waist. [Photo 71]

Bring the head and chest as close to the ground as you can.

With legs still spread, lean the upper body to the right and extend the right arm as far as possible along the inside of the right leg. Grab the big toe if possible with the first two fingers while extending the left arm overhead and to the right. [Photo 72]

Do the reverse to the other side.

The legs are still spread wide as you place the right hand on the floor behind the back and the left hand on the outer right thigh and twist from the waist all the way up through the head to the right.
[Photo 73] 
Do the reverse on the other side.

Bend the right leg so the heel touches the left buttock. Lift the left leg over the right.
With the left knee pointing up, place the heel of the left leg to the outside of the right knee. Place the right hand over the left knee. Put the left hand on the ground behind the tailbone and twist the torso and head to the left.
[Photo 74]

Do the reverse and twist to the right.

Extend the legs wide again.
Turn to the right and bend over the right leg reaching the hands toward the foot. Try to touch the head to the knee. [Photo 75]

Do the reverse to the left side.
Lie on your back with legs extended. Let your legs relax and rotate out.

Relax your arms at your sides, palms up. Close your eyes and relax. [Photo 76]

Feel the energy flowing through your body.

FURTHER DOWN THE PATH

You are being let in on a big secret. This shouldn't be a secret, but it is: 'enlightened' and 'relaxed' mean the same thing. They are synonymous. We are easing into liberation of the full expression of 'Self'. If you had the capacity to fully let go, you would literally fall into the full perfect expression of your being. Since enlightenment is so infrequent, the ability to completely relax appears to be very rare.

Asana is helping us to be at ease in our bodies so the body is no longer a distraction. Pranayama is helping create the necessary energy and balance. Now we can start to relax. We can meditate.

MEDITATION

Meditation can take many forms. Indeed, each time you meditate is original, even if you employ a technique again and again. As we practice meditation, our meditation evolves. There are many ways to meditate. The technique employed with this teaching is an efficient method of accomplishing the goals set forth in the teaching. You are encouraged to try other techniques and experience what they have to offer.

The natural result of the meditation suggested with this teaching is that the total being comes into healthy balance and obstructions to the flow of life force energy are cleared. As a result, the body is able to correct irregularities such as excess weight, as it is no longer obstructed from its optimum expression.

When this happens, the natural result is spiritual growth. There are no distinct borders where the body ends and the mind starts, the mind ends and the spirit begins. For the approach to work, it must be holistic, working at all levels at the same time.

Awareness is amplified. Meditation allows us to bathe in the growing awareness. It allows us to relax enough to feel the body, to observe the working of the mind, and be aware of the increasing joy immersing our spirit. The opportunity to meditate should be anticipated with gladness. It is chance to place everything in proper perspective. Not only is the chatter of the mind stilled, the issues which capture your attention are appreciated for their real significance. It is like reshuffling a deck of cards to deal your self the perfect hand.

Spiritual growth takes a lot of energy. The yogi is trying to conserve energy, create more energy, and direct life force towards higher goals. Meditation can make us much more efficient. The time we devote to meditation is paid back many times over. The importance of being aware enough to see what is really going on can't be overstated. A lot of time and effort can be squandered when viewing reality from a diminished perspective.

KUNDALINI

In the Hindu yoga tradition, Kundalini is a beautiful metaphor for unimpeded flow of energy from the lowest depths of the base of the spine to beyond the crown of the skull into the realm of the divine. The Kundalini experience relies on universal body structures and has been encountered by mystics throughout the ages. The imagery reflects the occult principle of the body as the microcosm echoing the large configuration of the macrocosm. Shakti, the cosmic feminine principle, combines in perfect union (yoga) with Shiva, the masculine cosmic principle to create perfect balance.

Latent Kundalini energy, potent negatively charged apana, reposes in the lowest esoteric center of the body. Pictured as a serpent coiled in the area analogous to the tailbone, it blocks the portal to liberation, the Sushumna.

The sleeping coiled serpent is awakened by the tapas (heat of devotion) of the yogi. The female goddess, in her serpent form, then begins to uncoil opening the door of the channel to the Absolute. The yogi, utilizing the skills learned though much sincere and diligent practice, entices the Kundalini energy up the spine through the Sushumna. Each successive chakra is entered and aroused, provoking full expression of each chakra's distinctive attributes and further encouraging the ascent, until the crown of the head is pierced and the thousand-petal lotus is entered. This is the locus of the static point of the positive, masculine psycho-spiritual energy, the male god, Shiva. This is complete union, the fullest expression of yoga, perfect and unique to yoga. Unlike other spiritual practices, it includes the body. Not only is the mind transcended, the body is illuminated and experienced as the body of the divine. The physical plane is entwined in the higher realms. The ideal of liberation combines with worldly enjoyment.

SENSUALITY

The closer we are to God, the more pleasurable our experience is. When the body is toned and tuned it vibrates waves of wellbeing. Just as pain is the body's means of letting us know something is wrong, joyous physicality signals when things are as they should be. When we are balanced and healthy, being is a sensual experience.

Fecundity is the order of our universe. Life fostering consciousness welcomes every opportunity to be. The consciousness of single-celled life forms navigate existence by being chemically attracted to that which brings pleasure and avoiding chemical sensations of distress and pain. Life is an erotic experience.

The lessons we are learning on the physical plane are the reasons for our existence on this plane. Those lessons can only be learned here. Our physical form is the utility for the necessary experiences. We are divided into gender, male and female. Sex shouldn't be treated as a hindrance to enlightenment or spiritual wholeness, but recognized as a microcosmic expression of the macrocosmic duality that animates our universe. The relationship represented by the yin yang symbol shows the 'one' being made aware of its self through interaction with the 'other', forming the 'whole'.

Yoga reveres balance, and sexual union is the balance of opposites, a manifestation of our divine nature. Sex is sacred, not against God, not a sin. The yogi is God loving rather than God fearing. The yogi chooses to embrace his or her nature rather than deny it. If you call a healthy, natural expression of life a sin, then you can expect to live in a perpetual state of guilt.

The word for sex in Sanskrit is 'kama', as in Kama Sutra, the classic seventh century manual on lovemaking. Kama translates as 'love-sex together'. Sex and love are entwined in one concept. Kama is also a name for the Hindu goddess of love. The early appeal of yoga in the United States in the nineteenth and twentieth centuries was imbued with sexual titillation. Generally, modern followers of Hinduism in India are even more sexually repressed than most Westerners. That's saying a lot, since many of us live in a state of frustrated sexual over-stimulation. The sacred is perverted to the carnal and our unfulfilled natural desires are subverted to marketing tools.

Sexual frustration is an expression of imbalance that the mind often attempts to correct with the intake of food. The fallacy of this is obvious when recognized. The love-sex expressed by 'kama', as opposed to rutting, has that most important of all elements–love. Touch, as an expression of love, is so important to our being, that infants can wither and die without it. Studies in nursing homes have discovered that even the touch of a pet can foster healthier wellbeing. We live in a wasteland of disconnection. Prakriti, everything but the divine, is always in a state of change. Through yoga, we can give positive direction to that change.

The practice of yoga awakens the sensual being that is in each of us. Being able to love one's self is necessary in order to love others. Loving others is necessary to be able to love one's self. Each of us can work with what we have–the power to change our self–and every life that touches ours will be affected by our love.

GNOSTIC CREATION

Gnostic Christians shared a beautiful creation myth that proclaims a much more loving God than the Old Testament deity. The Absolute is seen as very distant from this world. Other divine manifestations were created as companions to the Absolute. The youngest of these divinities was Sophia. Out of curiosity, she looked away from the Absolute into the void and wondered how far it went. She dived into the void and dove further and further. After a long time, she realized how far away from the Absolute she was and shuddered with anguish. The energy of that shudder formed our universe.

According to the Sophia myth, the Old Testament God, the god of this universe, is the product of the energy of that shudder of anguish and is a lesser god. That is why the Hebrews portrayed him as a vengeful and a frightening deity, and it explains why some people were said to be favored over others (an imbalance). That is why he ordered followers to murder other peoples, killing even women and children. Women were seen as less than men (an imbalance) and then blamed for the imbalance (sin) that keeps humans from heavenly grace.

Even the energy of that shudder is of the Absolute and the Absolute won't forsake any particle of its whole. It is Sophia's duty to bring everything back into the fold. To accomplish the resurrection, she has helped the spiritual growth of humanity by fostering teachers, many of whom we consider the great religious leaders of history.

Jesus is seen as one of these teachers, an expression of God, as everything is of God, but not 'the God'. The Hebrews have a history of looking for a messiah, someone to make things right. For most, this was sought in the form of a political leader. The teachings of Jesus speak to a much deeper level of reform. He tried to show our true nature as children of, and part of, the divine. He demonstrated a personal relationship to the divine, direct access, with no priests as intermediaries. This communion with the divine was illustrated when the veil of the temple that covered the Holy of Holies (symbolically separating man from God) was torn open at the moment Jesus left his physical body during crucifixion. He taught that each person expressing true divine nature would reform the world. When his teachings are read personally, with the heart, they speak of love and how to realize our true spiritual identity. Gnosis, knowledge of God, is within each of us. The Gnostic scriptures are imbued with sensuality.

ORIGINS

There are similarities in the belief systems of the Celtic peoples (the first historical occupants of Europe north of the Mediterranean) and the beliefs of the Aryan peoples (settlers of Northern India 6000 years ago who fostered a continuous yogic tradition to the present). This is not a coincidence. Their roots in pre-history are from the same ancestors. Most of the ritual that was passed on orally by the Celts, who had written language but believed the sacred was profaned when recorded in writing, has been obscured by attempts of later cultures to erase their influence. The Aryans held the same belief in an exclusively oral spiritual tradition. The direct descendants of this Northern Indian culture still maintain this tradition and members of the Brahmin class are responsible for learning exact renditions of their spiritual observance and passing it on orally to the next generation. Before the Romans conquered them and the Holy Roman Church stamped out their beliefs as heresy, the Druids, the priest class of the Celts, maintained the oral heritage. Most of what is available of the Druid liturgy today was preserved by early Irish Christian monks, and much of the translated wording is almost the same as observances still repeated in the Indian spiritual legacy. Both cultures share a belief in reincarnation and many of the earliest artifacts are similar.

Most of the large rivers in Europe still have the names given them by the indigenous Celts. The rivers are named after their significant gods. The spread of Celtic hegemony chronicled the sequence of each deity's change in importance over time. The proto-deity of the earliest known Celts was named 'Don'. The predecessor god of the early Aryan civilization shared the same name. Anthropologists believe the Aryan people migrated into what is now Northern India and Pakistan from the steppes of Southern Europe. The ancestors of both cultures originally were the same people, living along the Don River in what is now Ukraine. The myths of both civilizations tell of their ancestors' origin in a land where there the nights lasted for days and then the days were long. We can speculate that before settling along the river Don, these ancestors migrated from above the Artic Circle.

CONSEQUENCES

The relationship between the Aryan and Celtic cultures demonstrates how Westerners are reacquainting culturally with a spiritual tradition once familiar to their early ancestors. How this information was selectively used in a negative manner in the middle of the last century also demonstrates the danger of so-called knowledge as opposed to understanding.

The anthropological discoveries of the 1920's, in what was then Northern India, were used as propaganda by a political movement that gained control in Germany. The country was in disarray following World War I. The pride of the German people was devastated by their defeat and by the heavy-handed reparations demanded by the victors. A political party, playing to the damaged self-image of the German people, told them they were the descendants of this once great ancient Aryan civilization and genetically superior to others who didn't share this heritage. Germany conquered much of Europe and portrayed people of other ethnic backgrounds as inferior to the German people. As a result, millions of innocent civilians were systematically slaughtered. This shortsighted tendency to divide 'us' from 'them' has persisted since small bands of primitives fought over limited food resources. Constructs such as race, religion and tribalism further the history of reciprocal destruction that torments humankind.

Awareness of our true nature exposes these distinctions to be as foolish as they are fateful. If a soul is incarnated as a Chinese peasant one lifetime, a German schoolteacher the next, and then an Israeli Jewish Rabbi, or any conceivable variation of incidental lives, anything but spiritual growth is just a myopic preoccupation. We often think of reincarnation following a linear sequence like history or time; this isn't necessarily so. What if you were a torturer in the Spanish Inquisition one incarnation and a tortured heretic (in the same time period) in the next life?

What goes around comes around.

The Israelis, many of whom were survivors of the German Holocaust, are now treating the Palestinians as if they were inferior, dehumanizing them as the 'other'. This type of behavior isn't exemplary of any religious or ethnic group, but it is an example of the way unrealized humans conduct themselves.

Males have subjugated women in most cultures, unaware that gender can vary with incarnations. Even if individuals can't project their awareness far enough to embrace the Oneness that is all, self-interest should enforce the Golden Rule–do unto others as you would have done unto yourself.

KARMA

The concept of karma reflects the inter-connective relationship of everything. The mind tends to differentiate perception into separate objects of attention, when everything is actually touching and integrated with everything else. An action 'here' has an effect on 'over there', no matter how subtle. This cohesion exists from the minute subatomic particles to the galaxies. Every action evokes a reaction. Sanskrit 'karma' translates to 'action' in English. Everything we do has consequences. We've come to popularly refer to this as our 'karma'. All creatures have experiences in accordance with their karma. Karma is the force that propels us through cycles of life and death. Life can be pictured as a waterwheel, and karma as the water that keeps the wheel spinning. This is exemplified in the concept of the 'Wheel of Life', a symbol of Buddhism.

One's fate is determined by the quality of one's being in past lives and in the present life. Circumstance is a result of the moral force of a person's intentions, thoughts, and behaviors. Even the moral dimension of an individual's existence is causally determined. For example, the parents a person is born to influence the values a child will learn.

How can the nexus of moral causation be escaped? The nature of existence is activity. Even abstention is a form of action. The yogi acts without postulating a subjective center, without ego. This is liberation. Cultivating a self-transcending disposition arrests the vicious circle of karma. Spiritual practice can diffuse bad karma and create good karma.

RITUAL

The prescribed order of morning practice is a ritual. The suggested sequence is "purposeful striving", designed to efficiently achieve transformation. Dedication and commitment are spawned by the results.

ASSISTANCE

Gurdjieff, a meta-physicist in the first half of the twentieth century, talked of "feeding the angels". He said beings more spiritually advanced than humans, living on a subtle higher plane of existence, rely upon us for sustenance. Nature has complex organisms subsist on less complex forms – a food chain. When humans strive for transformation (Gurdjieff called this "conscious labor and intentional suffering" – he had a sense of humor) we give off vibrations of a certain frequency that nourish these higher forms of consciousness. When people are diligent and consistent in their efforts toward spiritual growth, becoming a reliable source of these indispensable vibrations, they gain the higher beings' attention. A person's intense and proper devotion causes the advanced entities to actively become involved in the wellbeing of the person. Self-interest encourages the higher forms of consciousness to take an active part in promoting their human benefactors' success.

DIVINE BREATH

The teaching has encouraged a breath pattern of breathing 'out' for twice as long as the time spent breathing 'in', with a pause following the 'in' breath. The pause, named the kumbhaka in Sanskrit, is one of the most direct means of effecting changes in consciousness. This is an extremely efficient way of breathing that balances, relaxes and stimulates the higher centers of the brain. Once comfortable with this breathing pattern, it can be more refined. With practice, the acolyte can start to breathe out for eight counts, breathe in for four counts, and retain the breath for two counts of eight. This may present some difficulty at first, but it becomes second nature with practice. Initiating this breath is most difficult in times of stress or duress, but that is when it is most rewarding. Beginners may experience some discomfort at first, feeling they cannot get enough air. But if they persist, this sensation will soon pass as the breathing starts to relax the mind and body. This is the ultimate pranayama. It mirrors the sequential repetition of inception for the cosmos, earning the title, "Divine Breath".

On a practical level, Divine Breath creates energy. If an enterprise requiring extreme exertion is looming, the sequence can be practiced to invigorate and store reserves of strength. It is effective as a means of defusing nervousness and gaining clarity before an interview or conflict. The inebriate can employ Divine Breath to regain equilibrium. It removes the practitioner from the experience of physical and mental pain. Performed on occasion during the course of the day, untold benefits will be discovered.

On a deeper level, as the name would suggest, Divine Breath brings the practiced closer to God. As breath control is performed, the body and mind relax.

The body is more efficient. This affects the breath rate and breathing slows. As the breathing slows, it creates more relaxation. The accomplished yogi begins to use the heart beat as the metronome to count the breaths. As the yogi gets even more relaxed, the heart rate begins to drop. At a point of relaxation, the need to breathe is no longer felt. Breath is suspended. An attempt to describe the state of consciousness obtained would be inadequate.

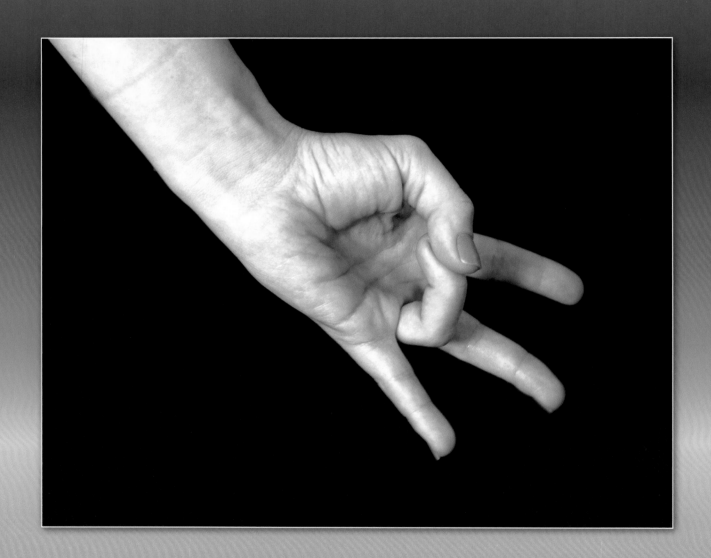

TOOLS TO AID YOUR PRACTICE

MUDRAS

From Sanskrit, mudra translates as seal, sign, or gesture. Mudras can be thought of as energetic connections made by consciously positioning parts of the body. Changing mudras can be compared to changing the wiring on a circuit board to alter the path of electrical currents. The circuit of the life force energy, prana, can be manipulated to accomplish desired influences with an understanding and employment of beneficial body configurations.

Given time and experimentation, you can discover some of these both positive and negative arrangements of the body for yourself. Once you have become aware of the concept and start to pay attention, you may notice you are unconsciously doing this all the time. If you get into a position that feels uncomfortable, not necessarily physically, but psychically, you change it. You do this without thinking. Careful observation shows the various circuits conducting life force energy can influence and even permanently alter body function.

Many beneficial ways of configuring the body, referred to in yoga as mudras, have been known through the ages and examples can be seen represented in the dance and art of many cultures. Even the common act of placing the palms together in prayer is a mudra, the Prayer or Anjali Mudra. The palms held together are the meeting place of yin and yang, symbolizing the completeness of the Divine. The Prayer Mudra is also called the Namaste Mudra when used to acknowledge the Divine in all.

We are going to explore a few mudras that have features that promote the stated goals of this practice. Mudras are a science and you are encouraged to delve further into this pragmatic study, the knowledgeable execution of which can greatly influence your health and wellbeing.

First we'll discuss the Shiva Tongue Mudra. When meditating, softly hold the tip of the tongue to the roof of the mouth. With the attention on the Third Eye Chakra, awareness of the position of the tongue is more pronounced.

The tip of the tongue can be drawn further back along the roof of the mouth. This creates an energetic connection that stimulates the production of beneficial brain chemicals such as melatonin, serotonin, and the endorphins. In the yoga lexicon, all these beneficial brain chemicals are lumped together and called "Amrita", Sanskrit for "Heavenly Nectar". In some yoga traditions the drawing back of the tongue, even into the opening of the floor of the nasal cavity, is described as tasting or savoring the Amrita, thought of as dripping from above. Some aspirants would go so far as to slice the flesh holding the front of the tongue to the floor of the mouth freeing the tongue to probe further up into the nasal cavity. Various results are reported in some of the arcane yoga literature–which of course can only be validated by experience. It is suggested this practice be considered an example of carrying what might be constructive on one level, too far. Yoga reveres balance and extremes upset balance. Part of the learning that proceeds from a balanced practice, without striving, is that 'more' often isn't better; simply stated, 'enough' is enough.

Convenient and often universal types of mudras are those formed with the hands. Examples of the universality of these expressions abound. Think of the North American Native Peoples sharing the outfacing raised palm as a symbol of peace and the art and statuary from all over the world that exhibit the same gesture as expressing peace and good intention. Raising the open outfaced palm causes the one performing the mudra to feel benign intent on an energetic level that transcends cultural boundaries.

In the chapter "Getting Started" three of the most useful mudras were presented. The first was the Grounding Mudra, Prithvi Mudra [Photo 15]. The tip of the thumb and the ring finger are held together. This can be done on one or both hands. The effect is to ground the individual to the matter beneath them and to all the history and factors that place them in this moment in time and space. As with all the mudras, many influences are felt that effect mood and the physical body but we will focus on the effects relevant to this practice. It is  left to the observer performing the mudra to identify other effects. The yogi will intuit these connections, and nothing trumps self-discovery.

The Grounding Mudra was shown with the palms turned down. Many of the hand mudras can be performed with the palms facing up or facing down, creating a different energetic effect. Palms down causes more introspection and is especially effective when directing energy to achieve grounding. We are all in different places in terms of our objectives, and at different times these change for the individual. Intuition is the best guide to what will fulfill our current needs. Trust yourself and listen to the guru within. In the course of the day, if a situation arises that causes you to feel unsure or spacey, the Grounding Mudra will foster inner stability and self-assurance. It strengthens the body and mind and increases energy.

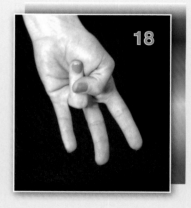

The Morning Practice next employs the Sun Mudra, Suyra Mudra [Photo 18]. In this mudra the ring finger is laid across the palm for its full length and the thumb is placed over it, firmly holding the ring finger down. The effects of this mudra are noticeable; heat is created in the body. The metabolism is accelerated and body fat is burned. The practitioner is urged to drink large amounts of water to prevent dehydration. This mudra is good to help you realize how powerful and effective the mudras actually are. The Sun Mudra seems so simple and isn't intrusive, so it is easy to underestimate its effectiveness until it is personally experienced. An effort over a reasonably short time produces noticeable results. If you can relax enough and pay attention, you can actually feel it working. The mudra can be performed whenever your hands are free, and can be done in such a way that no one else need be aware of what you are doing. Again, be warned against striving. Utilize the mudra with restraint and you will observe it is more effective when employed with awareness. Find your own balance and remember–more isn't necessarily better. We each have our individual cycles and optimum rate for healthy transformation.

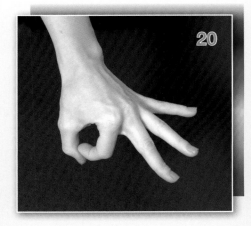

Next the Morning Practice describes and utilizes the Peace, or Gyan, Mudra. [Photo 20] It is formed by placing the index finger on the crease made by the joint of the thumb. In some traditions the thumb represents God, the index finger represents 'man', and the placement of the index finger along the length of the thumb represents man's relationship to God. Placing the index finger low on the length of the thumb can be thought of as showing man as humble. This *Jewel in the Lotus* teaching splits the difference, placing the index finger half way along the thumb and represents seeing God in all.

This is a very powerful mudra for the sense of wellbeing it reflects in the user. The Peace Mudra is very comfortable. It empowers spirituality and mental tranquility and relieves stress, depression, and insomnia. It is often a first introduction to developing extra sensory abilities such as telepathy and clairvoyance. The Peace, or Gyan, Mudra engenders realization beyond the expectations of our cultural boundaries.

Another very peaceful mudra is the Heart, or Anahata Mudra. The upturned palms rest in the lap with the thumbs away from the body. [Photo 78] Men place the right hand on top and women will place the left hand over the right. This isn't a sexist motivated differentiation. It neutralizes gender by placing the dominant energy cradled in and dependent for support on the hand representing the qualities of the other gender. Sometimes called the Green Mudra, the Heart Mudra reflects the qualities of the Fourth Chakra and engenders a relaxed sentiment of all-pervading love. As well as strengthening the capacity for compassion, a tenderhearted sensibility fosters readiness to let down barriers in an atmosphere of openness–the ability to let go and feel.

The changing and control of eating habits is assisted by the use of the Rudra Mudra. The Mudra is formed by placing the tips of the index finger and the ring finger on the top of the thumb with the others fingers extended comfortably. [Photo 79] The Rudra Mudra can be thought of as the "What Should I Eat" Mudra. When ordering in a restaurant or thinking, "Should I have dessert?" or dishing up your plate, employ the Rudra Mudra to assist eating for need rather than eating out of habit or for sublimated fulfillment. Perform the mudra and think about what you are going to eat, and the act of eating will be in a clearer perspective. Timing is important, but with practice the Rudra Mudra can be one of the acts you perform habitually when taking sustenance.

The subject of enlisting mudras for weight control isn't complete without mentioning the Linga or Weight Reduction Mudra. The palms are joined in front of the chest while locking facing fingers together and holding the thumbs upright. [Photo 80] After holding for three minutes reverse and have the opposite index finger on top and hold for another three minutes. This mudra is important for its ability to reprogram the metabolism by increasing the metabolic rate. It should not be performed more than twice on each side per day. It is most effective when each series is performed at different times, for example, once in the morning and once at night. Consistent practice over a period of time will affect permanent change in the metabolic rate. The Linga Mudra is encouraged for the permanent results, even though it works slowly and cannot be easily performed without arousing the attention of others.

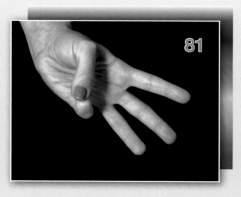

Another mudra that demands mention is the Varuna or Beauty Mudra, formed by placing the thumb over the tip of the little finger and keeping the remaining three fingers comfortably straight. [Photo 81] A feminine mudra, It has some fat reducing effectiveness, moisturizes the skin and helps relieve menstrual cramps.

A helpful mudra that is often used in conjunction with the asanas, especially those utilizing the arms extended overhead, is the Kali or Completion Mudra. It is formed by extending the index fingers while the other fingers and thumbs are inner-twined. [Photo 82] The Completion Mudra signifies mastery.

The last hand mudra presented is the Shiva Linga Mudra, an upturned fist with thumb extended resting on

an open palm. [Photo 83] It represents the unimaginable power of creativity that existed before "All" was brought into being and is modeled on the Shiva Linga, an object of Hindu spiritual adoration that resembles a phallus as it would appear from the vantage point of the womb during sexual penetration. The Shiva Linga Mudra engenders strength, determination, and spiritual clarity. Women make the mudra with the left hand on top while men have the right hand above.

It should be kept in mind the mudras are tools to aid your practice. The foundation of your transformation is the ritual of the Morning Practice and although the mudras have effectiveness standing alone, they are to be used in conjunction with the whole teaching. We are always looking for shortcuts, but in order to get optimum results, you must be willing to do the work. Very little is being asked of the participant considering the priceless dividends. A criticism of our culture is the unrealistic expectation of "something for nothing." Gird your loins and get with the project. It is holistic, and for maximum results the practice must be undertaken in its complete form.

BANDHAS

Another tool for managing energy in the body are the bandhas. Often described as energy locks, a more appropriate term would be energy valves. Bandha, in Sanskrit, translates as "bond." Energy isn't dammed up or constricted, but directed inward and upward. When used during asana, pranayama, and meditation, the bandhas prevent energy from dissipating. Bandhas influence energy flow towards the spinal column and up to the higher spiritual centers. On a gross level, the effectiveness of the bandhas can be realized when holding difficult or tiring yoga postures. This conservation of energy allows the practitioner to sustain a posture longer. The art of employing bandhas can be learned doing asana and then applied on more subtle levels, where their value is even more pronounced.

Employing a bandha is primarily a psychic, rather than physical, endeavor. One way to describe activating a bandha is to think of a slight vacuum on the interior of the bandha's location. This ever so slight sensation of negative pressure is more conceptual than physical. Individuals further along in their spiritual development employ bandhas continuously, often as a form of unconscious body discipline.

The lowest bandha, referred to as the root lock, or Mula Bandha, is located at the perineum, the region of the body between the anus and the scrotum or vulva. Ascending the spine, behind the diaphragm is the flying upward, or Uddiyana, Bandha. Third is the throat valve, or Jalandhara Bandha, located at the base of the throat. When beginners set this third bandha in asana, the chin is often tilted on to the chest.

Bandhas are important because directing and conserving energy are helpful to experience states of intense spiritual awareness. The aspirant begins by employing the bandhas during asana practice and with diligence will come to understand their subtleties. All three bandhas can be used at the same time. This is called Tribandha. Ideally, when pranayama is performed, Tribandha should be applied.

PRANAYAMA

Breath control, or pranayama, is a primary tool for the yogi. In the previous section, we discussed breath as a bridge between the sympathetic and parasympathetic nervous systems. We also discussed and explained Divine Breath–a crown jewel of this teaching. Awareness of the breath is possibly the most consistent means of establishing pratyahara, or withdrawal from the senses. With constant use over time, forms of controlled breathing can become habitual and their benefits produced while no longer requiring conscious attention.

One form of pranayama we've grown familiar with through the Morning Practice is Breath of Fire – quick exhalations through the nose, pulling in the stomach and diaphragm, with a passive inhalation. Some schools of yoga call this quick exhalation and passive inhalation through the nose Skull Shining, or Kapalabhati Breath and use the name Breath of Fire only when the breath is through the mouth.

Alternate Nostril Breathing is universally called Nadi Shuddhi, but it is performed in many variations. The style taught in the Morning Practice is most effective for the objective of that ritual.

Victorious Breath, Ujayi, can be incorporated into asana practice. You breathe so the breath is purposefully audible. The breath resonates in the back of the throat nose and mouth in such a way as to resemble the sound of waves and wind at an ocean beach. As well as maintaining attention on the breath, Victorious Breath energizes and strengthens the physical body.

Humming Bee, or Bhramari Breath is performed with the jaw closed, teeth touching, while making a sound like a bumble bee in flight by vibrating, at varying pitch, the partially closed lips. Apart from the pleasant tingling vibration through out the skull, the breath tunes you in to a region of the psyche deep behind the third eye called the Cave of the Bumble Bees; a portal to Universal Consciousness.

Bellows, or Bhastrika Breath, is performed breathing in and breathing out deeply and rapidly through the open mouth. It is done for a short time and when the participant begins to get dizzy, it is suspended, then taken up again when the dizziness disappears. It grounds you in the present, can cause sexual arousal, and creates reserves of oxygen in the blood.

> *Breath control, or pranayama, is a primary tool for the yogi.*

Another practical breathing tool is the Cooling, or Sitali Breath. This breath operates on the same principle as a dog panting. Short breaths are rapidly passed, almost fluttered, over the top of the tongue. (Animals that don't perspire through their skin, such as dogs, use a similar breath pattern to control their body temperature.) The effect is enhanced if you can curl your tongue up on the sides, using the edges of the mouth to create a depression along the line of the center of the tongue's length. Ten percent of us aren't genetically wired to do this and will have to settle for just making an "O" shape with the lips.

Another variation of the Cooling Breath is Sitkari Breath. Here the lips are held open with the teeth touching and you breathe in through the mouth, over the tongue, and back out through the nose.

DRISHTI

Your drishti is your point of focus. This can be on two levels; focus regarding what you are visually looking at and/or focused on, and what is held in the mind's eye. To assist with balance while performing the physical postures of asana, the practitioner often will look at some stationary object. This is the most common use of the word in western yoga culture.

In another form of drishti, some yoga aspirants will gaze at the tip of their nose or look up at their brow above and between the eyes, concentrating on these points during meditation. If curiosity compels you to try this out, you can judge what, if any, contribution this creates, and if it has personal benefit.

During the meditation part of the ritual we've named the Morning Practice, you are asked to gently close your eyes. With the eyes closed, the screen of the imagination is open for business. To supersede distraction, at the level of each chakra you are told to flood the screen with a color. This flood of color is multi-functional, but one consequence is withdrawal of the senses. Each color exists at a different vibrational frequency and acts like a tuning fork.

Try to locate the screen. Some suggest it is about two inches behind the brow, but another way of perceiving the field of the mind's eye can be as other dimensional.

You are still affected by outside physical stimulus when your eyes are closed. For example, you'll notice the influence of bright light filtering through the eyelids. So even if the focus is held within, there is connection to the body kosha and the physical plane. Everything is interconnected, a part of the field, where you are is where you place yourself in the field. This is your reality. 'All' is there. Where you are in that 'All' determines the reality you are experiencing.

> *"Out beyond ideas of wrong doing and right doing, there is a field. I'll meet you there."*
> *- Rumi*

In Sanskrit, some of the translations of drishti are gaze, view, and opinion. Another beauty of Sanskrit, as the language of transformation, is the ability to form a concept by considering the different ways the same word is used.

Where should your gaze be? Make yourself comfortable and place your right hand, with index finger extended upward, directly in front of the bridge of the nose. Take the left hand, also with the index finger raised and hold it about six inches forward of the right hand. With the eyes, look first at the closer right hand. Then look at the left hand. Shift the attention of the eyes back and forth from one index finger to the other.

preventing the common cold

Now place the right hand, with the index finger still raised at the back of the skull at a height in line with the eyes. Place the left hand, index finger raised, directly in line with, but six inches behind the right. With the mind's eye, look from the right to the left index finger several times.

Next place the right hand where the left previously was, and the left hand yet another six inches behind that. With the mind's eye, look from the right to the left extended index finger. Take note of the location of the inner vision while focused on the left index finger at the greatest distance.

Put the hands down and repeat the drill using only the mind. That point you've identified at the furthest back position of the tip of the left index finger is the ideal point of focus. This is your inner drishti.

IRRIGATING THE NOSE

Recently, the University of Southern California released the results of a multi-year study on the common cold. The researchers said their findings showed that the most effective means of preventing the common cold was a five thousand year old yoga technique–irrigating the nose. As well as cleaning the sinuses and nasal passages, the technique was credited by the study with boosting the immune system. Water is simply flushed through the nose and down through the back of the throat to the mouth. The remaining moisture is then expelled by blowing the nose.

Although any clean water can be used, the procedure is done more comfortably if a little salt, preferably sea salt, is added to the water. The approximate mixture is a pinch of salt to a cup of water. Experimentation will reveal the correct blend for you. If the salt is too concentrated, a burning sensation will be felt. If there is too little salt, the sensation will be like getting water up your nose at the swimming pool. It is suggested once you find the correct formula, mix up a couple weeks supply in a small bottle. Have it ready in the medicine cabinet and form the habit of irrigating your nose, once on each side, each morning after brushing your teeth.

In India, a neti pot, a small container that looks like a flower watering pot with a very curved spout, delivers the liquid into the nostril with the head tilted back. Members of the

U.S.C. study suggested the use of a small pump to deliver the salty water. Both are examples of the human tendency to complicate an otherwise simple process.

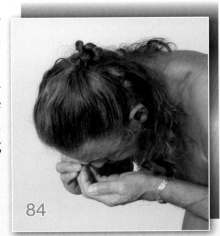

The cleansing liquid can simply be poured into a cupped palm. The fingers of the other hand can cover and block one nostril and the liquid be sucked up into the open nostril. [Photo 84] This should be done slowly. Continue drawing air up into the nostril after all the liquid has been drawn in for a slow count of twenty to allow saturation of the sinuses. Fill the other palm with liquid and repeat the procedure using the other hand, and inhaling with the other nostril. Unless you have problems with blocked nasal passages, this need be done only one time on both sides each day.

A further refinement involves placing the little fingers in the nasal openings sealing them. Then a quick pulsing breath begins, inflating and releasing the air in the nasal passages. This should be done for twenty-four cycles. This acts to clean the sinuses. [Photo 85]

Next hold the jaw slackly open and place the tips of the index fingers where the jaw meets the skull. Start a circular motion rubbing along the cheekbone. [Photo 86] This will make your ears pop. Continue doing this for several seconds moving the fingers along the top of the cheekbone. Notice the subtle difference of the popping in different locations and when rotating

opposite directions. Doing this daily will prevent your Eustachian tubes from gradually sealing shut, which can happen with age, causing hearing loss.

Blow your nose and know you've greatly increased the odds that you will not get ill.

SPECIAL CIRCUMSTANCES

A person paralyzed with spinal cord injuries can experience the physical, mental and spiritual transformation resulting from a sincere yoga practice. Some of us are destined to live this incarnation under special circumstances. The meaning of life is the same. Our purpose is to grow into the highest expression of our true self. Realizing the relative unimportance and transitory nature of the physical body– seeing that its 'wants' need to be tamed in order to concentrate awareness so we may achieve our fullest expression–provides comfort. All of us have limitations and must work within those boundaries. A part of the attitude towards life expressed in the Santosa Niyama is acceptance. Sometimes this is harder for persons living under what are considered 'normal' physical circumstances to appreciate. To do the best we can is the full expression of our karma (action). A sincere effort is required to experience what it is we should be learning now. Everything that is prakriti is in a constant state of change. With yoga, we give direction to that change.

sincere effort required

Feldenkrais practitioners who work with individuals who have lost some of their physical capabilities have made some interesting observations. When one side of the body is compromised, if the other side is exercised, the unused side benefits in a sympathetic relationship. When one loses use of part of the body, if they imagine the limb functioning, the damaged limb recovers function sooner. Thinking of doing actions, without actually doing them, engages the muscles that would have participated in the imagined action.

One can be so overweight that very little body movement is possible. If the extremely overweight person devotes the same time it would take to actually perform the actions to imagine performing them, the body will respond and receive benefit. If there is some part of the practice that is impossible for you, do what parts you can and form mental pictures for the actions that are not physically possible. The nerves and muscles will respond and the body will tone until the movement can be performed physically.

Be patient with yourself, and be persistent. If the action can't be done exactly as you think it should be done, modify the action and do it as best you can. The human body is amazing in its ability to learn and transform. None of us are perfect and everything is relative. On all levels, but especially spiritually, sincerity is what propels our advancement.

If a person is so naturally limber that the most difficult postures are easy for them, they are actually at a disadvantage. Much of the benefit comes from learning, from exerting the will and overcoming obstacles. Performing like an acrobat might impress others but it brings shallow recompense.

YOGA NIDRA

In the days when students would study yoga under the tutelage of a master for years, the last thing the master would often teach was Yoga Nidra. It is such a powerful tool, the guru would be sure the acolyte was sufficiently ensconced in the Eight Limbs to handle its powers wisely. The Walt Disney cartoon of the *Sorcerer's Apprentice* illustrates the folly of someone exercising powers they haven't earned and don't understand. However, this cartoon ignores a spiritual principle that acts as a safety valve. Natural Law denies the uninitiated access to powers they aren't ready to handle. Only when one knowingly uses power inappropriately can one do damage, and the damage is primarily done to him or her self.

Yoga Nidra allows the individual to interact consciously with Universal Consciousness, the source of everything. Intention is planted in Universal Consciousness and that intention manifests itself in our real world. We all drift to the margins of Universal Consciousness from time to time. We may relax enough that individual consciousness starts to dissolve into the sea of All. With awareness and training we can visit the source of the origins of our reality and help to form the future. We reclaim that portion of the Divine in everything that is the Creator.

A complete chapter is dedicated to Yoga Nidra. The chapter is presented as a Yoga Nidra session, first explaining what the practice is and how it works. The dialogue of a session is then presented. It is valuable to see the session in written form so it can be analyzed so the practitioner can understand its form–with the goal to mentally administer the practice on him or her self.

In many Western yoga classes a practice called Yoga Nidra is shared. Although what is done is a good first step towards true Yoga Nidra, the way it is being performed, it is little more than an effective relaxation technique. The full expression of the art results in the intentional forming of the future from the raw material of Universal Consciousness. Be sure you truly want what you ask for.

IN THE PRESENCE

Yoga Nidra as presented in this book was taught by Yogi Amirit Desai. If you feel it would be interesting or helpful to spend some time with a self-realized being, a true yoga guru of the Indian tradition, you might consider a pilgrimage to visit Yogi Amrit Desai. Known to his followers as Gurudev, he was a pioneer helping to bring yoga to America. He founded the Kripalu Yoga Center in Lennox, Massachusetts in the 1970's. Once the center was established and thriving, politics surrounding misinterpretation of morality at different levels of spiritual development, threatened destruction of the resource. Amrit Desai selflessly walked away from his creation that it might continue to spread the message of yoga.

The Kripala Yoga Center continues and prospers, albeit without its original inspiration, and Gurudev maintains a peaceful presence at the Amrit Yoga Institute in Salt Springs, Florida surrounded by those who appreciate the importance of the guru as a spiritual resource. Amrit is a lively man in his eighties, and with amazing vital energy and amiable goodwill, he makes himself available to those who want to share his presence. It is an important part of spiritual education to be around such a teacher, to see how exceptional, yet human, they are and to observe the people around the guru, to see how they relate to each other and to their teacher.

LET IT BE

In northeastern India, in the foothills of the Himalayas, the Tibetan government in exile resides in the city of Dharamsala. This is the home of the 14th Dalai Lama, Tenzin Gyatso, and in his temple complex, Suglag Khang, is a life-sized sculpture of Gautama before he became the Buddha. Although it is obvious, many people fail to make the connection: the Buddha is a yogi. He practiced a very austere form of yoga and the statue depicts him just before he threw in the towel on his self-depredation and learned to relax. The yogi is shown shortly before letting go, sitting under the Bodhi tree and experiencing enlightenment. He had subjected himself to such severe asceticism that he looks like a sunken-eyed, living skeleton.

Most know the story of the pampered Prince Siddhartha, born in 566 B.C., 2,500 years ago, in the small kingdom of Kapilavastu. Wise men predicted he would become a Buddha. His father wanted him to be a mighty ruler and tried to insulate Siddhartha from all the troubles of the world. He lived a life with every luxury until becoming disillusioned as a young man. Siddhartha walked away from his life of privilege and became a monk with the goal of finding a way to end suffering. He changed his name to Gautama and studied under many of the most advanced teachers. He lived in the forest, meditating and eating only roots, leaves, and berries. His life had swung from extreme privilege to extreme poverty. He had chosen to consume so little he was slowly dying.

After six years of hardship, he realized neither the life of luxury nor the life of an ascetic had brought him happiness. Overdoing doesn't lead to inner peace and spiritual freedom. He took nourishment to regain strength, and on a full moon in May he sat under the Bodhi tree in deep meditation. He vowed not to move until he received enlightenment. He finally relaxed enough to understand how things truly are. He gained supreme wisdom and became The Awakened One; he was Shakyamuni Buddha.

After enlightenment, he went to the Deer Park at the holy city of Benares and shared his new understanding with five holy men. They embraced the new Buddha's teaching immediately and became his disciples. For the next forty-five years Shakyamuni Buddha and his disciples traveled around India spreading the Dharma, his teachings. They relied on others for gifts of food and often slept on the ground, teaching and trying to improve the understanding of our true nature for all those who would listen.

According to one Buddhist tradition's history, in 486 B.C. Buddha gathered four of his most trusted monks. Realizing he was ready to pass, he taught them to meditate, to do exactly the meditation he experienced when he received enlightenment. He told them to go into seclusion and repeat the training, changing nothing. They, in turn, were to select a small trusted group and pass on the meditation with the same instructions, generation after generation, without allowing any slight change, until the time was right for the meditation to be taught widely. After centuries, the time is right to share the teaching, and those who are privileged to know the meditation (called Vipassana) are now doing what they can to share it with those interested. They selflessly provide ten-day silent retreats for those who want to learn the meditation.

Buddha knew he wasn't the first to become Buddha. Buddha was a title in India for someone who had reached enlightenment, just as the word Christ indicated a spiritual status in early Hebrew nomenclature. Shakyamuni Buddha told his followers, "There have been many Buddhas before me and will be many Buddhas in the future." He taught, "All living beings have the Buddha nature and can become Buddhas." To be Buddha, awake to your true nature. Relax into your self.

> *Two truths are common to many spiritual teachings: The Golden Rule, "Do unto others as you would have done unto yourself," and the promise, "Seek and you will find."*

Two truths are common to many spiritual teachings: the Golden Rule, "Do unto others as you would have done unto yourself," and the promise, "Seek and you will find." Now is the beginning of a great awakening. Humanity is ready to drop the encumbrances of our primitive origins. We are entering a new age, and each of us can embrace a new order. When we understand our true nature, we are no longer motivated by fear. We are to realize our birthright as children of God.

We live in a world of plenty and when those motivated by fear are no longer fearful and stop hoarding, there will be plenty for all. Few have selfishly amassed stores beyond their requirements for contentment, while others are left with nothing. If this terrible imbalance isn't corrected soon, such extreme instability will result in violent social upheaval. Once insecure individuals realize themselves, they'll see their excesses as a burden on their spirituality. Who wants to identify with 'things' when the material world is so transitory and the material offers no joy? Accumulation of wealth is another way of trying to fill a need that can only be satisfied by opening our hearts to the love that is our true nature. Soon everyone will come to understand why it was said, "It is harder for a rich man to get into heaven than for camel to pass through the eye of a needle." The closer we are to God, to our true nature, the more joyous our lives will be. Heaven is at hand. All we need do is let go of the encumbrances preventing us from relaxing into our full being. It is all here. It is just a matter of where we place our consciousness in it.

The awakening is going to happen whether you participate or not. The earth and what happens in other parts of the universe are interconnected, part of the field where every action anywhere affects everything everywhere. The cycle of influences the world is coming under will cause a shift into a new age, identified in western astrology as a shift from the Piscean Age to the Aquarian Age. In the Hindu nomenclature, we're leaving Kali Yuga, the dark age of spiritual ignorance that began with the death of Krishna in 3002 B.C.

Those that choose transformation will share joy, content-ment, and balance that, for most, was previously unimaginable. All things are brought forth through consciousness. Humanity is evolving to a new stage where spirituality is afforded stature above physical and mental powers.

Those who haven't yet got the message will see what is happening with their fellows who are doing the work to make this a better existence by improving themselves. We notice when others are peaceful and fulfilled. Greater awareness is accessible to all who are willing to make the effort.

This is a very simple teaching, and it is free, as all spiritual teachings should be. You don't have to join anything, pay dues, or tithe. You're not being asked to follow anyone as you rely on your own direct experience for all your answers.

> *Everyone is equal and motivation and direction come from inside.*

There is no 'us' and 'them'. Everyone is equal and motivation and direction come from inside. We're all going to make it. As told in the Sophia myth, God isn't going to leave any part of its Self behind. The only punishment we undergo is not having the greatest, most joyous, expression of or being – until we do have that more joyous expression – and then we see it as part of the learning process.

It is not surprising that God would love its Self and love each of us as expressions of that Self. Without awareness, the universe appears a chaotic, violent place in constant meaningless turmoil. Look inside to find meaning and peace. Doesn't God want to have a good time? Of course! We are the form the Divine has taken to enjoy, to be in joy. The kosha that most closely surrounds your true self, your spark of the Divine, is the Anandamaya Kosha, the bliss body. Go inside and experience that bliss. It is waiting for you to acknowledge it.

Don't feel sorry for those who don't get it. They will. Eventually everyone will go through a similar joyous process of self-discovery.

87

AND THEN

You have been doing the Morning Ritual and realize it is a routine you will follow to continue to experience the transformation you've come to understand as your life's true path. Here are some elements you might add to make your morning practice a little more interesting.

Before you start the routine, stand with hands in Prayer and take four deep breaths.

Then be aware of the Third Eye Center and image the drishti as described in the Tools chapter. Think of the hands positioned before the forehead and then in the two positions behind the head. Find the point of focus on the furthest back imagined finger and think, "Maintain focus on my inner drishti, point of awareness".

"Breathe; be aware of the breath. Breathe into sensation. Prana rides the breath".

"Be one with the teacher, be one with the guru: both inner and outer".

These thoughts are three expressions, or attempted descriptions, of the unexplainable: Samadhi.

Now think, "Relax, relax, relax, relax".

After six repetitions of the Sun Salutation as initially presented (three times for each side), incorporate Warrior I into the sequence after the beginning Runner's Lunge. [Photo 87]

Warrior I posture is executed by spinning the toes of the back right foot slightly out while in Runner's Lunge. The left knee remains bent as the arms swing out from the side and together overhead. The torso straightens with the hips square to the front. The outer edge of the right foot is pressed firmly to the ground; the back is arched, tailbone down; and the head is tilted up looking past the hands.

Next, flow into Chaturanga posture (yogic pushup) by bending at the waist and placing the weight on both hands and extending both legs. The body is held parallel to the ground supported by straight arms and the toes of the feet. [Photo 88]

Now bend the elbows and lower the knees, leading with the heart. Swing the chest close to the floor and forward. [Photo 89]

Straighten the arms and look upward while relaxing
the spine. Upward Dog. [Photo 90]

91

92

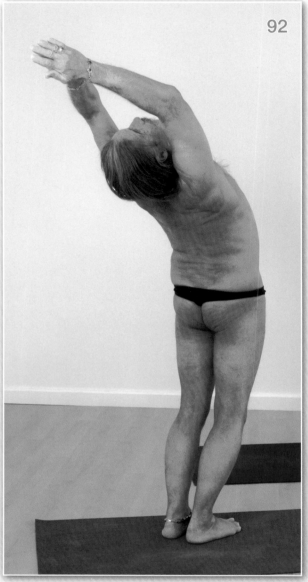

Continue the sequence, and upon standing upright with arms extended overhead, relax the lower back and bend backwards as far as comfortable. Back bending can be extremely beneficial. In our Western culture most bending motions are forward; hunching over a computer keyboard is an example. [Photos 91 and 92]

93

After doing the sequence on both sides, perform it again and add Warrior II after doing Warrior I. [Photo 93] In both Warrior Postures, keep the forward bent knee over the ankle. Have the hips square to the front. Hold the outer edge of the back foot pressed to the ground with the foot at a forty-five degree angle to the front. In Warrior II, shoulders should be relaxed and arms horizontal, stretching out through the fingertips. Look out over the front fingers with spine upright.

Complete the sequence on both sides with all the new modifications and then repeat again. This time add Warrior III. [Photo 94]

94

Begin by wind milling the back arm forward, from Warrior II extension, so it is parallel to and alongside the front arm. Feel the ground under the front foot with weight distributed evenly. Straighten that leg. Extend forward through both arms as the back leg is raised and extended horizontally while rolling the body parallel to the ground. Stretch forward through the fingertips with the palms together while extending back through the toes with the leg parallel to the ground. Look forward.

Do the complete enhanced sequence on both sides.

Other suggested postures:

Camel, a variation on back bending [Photo 95];

Eagle Posture enhances full body flexibility and balance. [Photo 96]

97

Headstand, to develop balance and increase blood flow to the brain [Photo 97].

While performing asana, if you must think, think about what you're doing. Keep in mind the Sanskrit translation of asana: seat. You are making the body a comfortable seat for meditation.

The following Yoga Nidra, in the voice of the author, is available online at jewelinthelotus.biz. There is no fee. Yoga Nidra involves trust, so the complete text is presented here. It is suggested that you read the text first and then listen to the recording.

YOGA NIDRA

If you are listening to this guided meditation with a group, arrange yourselves in rows parallel to the front of the room with your mats fore and aft, close enough together that you could reach out and touch the person next to you. Have your blanket within reach. Sit in a comfortable position. We are going to do Yoga Nidra, yogic sleep.

Let's start with a brief description of Yoga Nidra and what we'll be doing. Yoga Nidra is the world of the Third Eye, the plane beyond the five senses. Once you learn to enter this state, you gain access to a whole new perspective that cannot be obtained when you are functioning in the limited world of the time-space dimension. You can shift from the conflict of duality to the balance of integration. Everything in our conscious state is based in duality. Good and evil, hot and cold, pleasure and pain. In nature all is in balance from the clockwork of the heavens in the far reaches of the cosmos to the balance in every minute atomic particle. In our awake-conscious state, the mind is always stating preferences derived from duality. This creates imbalance. Even thoughts that seem positive, "Isn't she beautiful," "That's nice," "I feel so good," are an expression of duality, and inherent in duality is a bias, a judgment. This is a trap of the mental plane.

When our mind is conscious, brain waves are in the fastest of the four cycles that can be measured by an electroencephalograph: beta waves (12-30 Hz, or cycles per second). Measurements show the higher end beta cycles are where we experience anxiety, uneasiness, fight or flight reactions and separateness.

As soon as you close your eyes, and inwardly focus, you create the alpha pattern of brain waves (8-12 Hz). This produces the state of relaxation between sleep and wakefulness. The lower frequency of the alpha state allows increased receptivity. This is where super-learning takes place, alpha brain awareness. This is the 'twilight state', the drowsiness that follows the waking state and precedes the sleep state. This is the prevailing wave pattern in meditation.

Even slower are the theta waves (4-8 Hz). It is difficult to maintain awareness for any length of time in this state. It is a state in which awareness drifts in and out. It is characterized by expanded states of memory, enhanced creativity, insights of sudden understanding and realizations that drop out of nowhere. This is the space of dreams and REM. Healing and integration happens here. Theta is considered to be the doorway to the unconscious mind. Brain synchronization takes place in this state. There is a relaxing of the linear, analytical left-brain and openness to the intuitive, all-knowing right brain. It is where the subconscious is receptive to change learned behavior and attitudes.

The slowest brain wave pattern that exists is delta (0.1-4 Hz). This is our deep sleep state. Awareness is possible at this slowest brain wave function, but only for the most advanced yogis. It is here where one experiences unity and oneness.

Alpha and beta represent ego-mind that operates in the gross planes of duality and polarity. Theta operates on a more subtle soul level of individual being. Delta is evident of the impersonal unified state of being. It is the ultimate flowering of pure witness.

This witness-like state of delta is experienced in the deep sleep that is entered unconsciously where individual separate ego with all its past memories and future anticipations (the sense of 'I am') temporarily enters unity consciousness. In deep sleep you are unconscious of time and space, past and future, duality conflict, tensions, mental and emotional irritations, fears and addictions. This is a temporary state. In Yoga Nidra you learn to enter this progressively subtle state consciously.

As you become more and more integrated all the limitations, inhibitions and blockages that exist as a result of stress, fear, conflicts, emotional reactions and karmic patterning progressively lessen and eventually melt away.

The theta waves that occur in dreaming and the delta waves occurring in deep sleep can be produced with progressively deeper states of Yoga Nidra and meditation. This takes practice that will develop a stable witness state, which will also carry over into the normal waking state. This state of delta is the ultimate flowering of the eighth limb of yoga, Samadhi.

Consciousness is integrated into sleep. Sleep (sleep wave patterns) is amalgamated into consciousness.

> Consciousness is integrated into sleep.

Ordinarily the theta waves that occur during dreaming and delta waves that occur during deep sleep cannot be produced in a fully conscious state. This state can only be attained when you are able to enter mature witness, where you are freed from identification with ego, self-concepts, body, mind and emotions.

This integrated state is beyond waking, dreaming and deep sleep. In the waking state you are identified with your body, mind and ego; as a result you become the victim of all inhibitions, limitations and the suffering that comes through, mind and ego. Alpha and beta represent our connection to the physical world. Theta connects us with the subtle world, and delta with the causal realm. When you learn to progressively enter into the deeper and subtler brain waves through Yoga Nidra, you become more relaxed, more integrated, more expansive and more present. Eventually you shift out of identification with body, mind and ego and while conscious you are in a deep sleep (nidra) and an integrated state (yoga). All aspects of our being, gross and subtle, causal and physical, mental and spiritual are in complete synergy and harmony and you become one with the whole.

With Yoga Nidra we are simply getting out of the way. This allows the all-knowing intelligence that energizes the universe to come to the front. In this way the miraculous intelligence that makes a rose a rose, or a star perfectly original, or creates a child, becomes our intelligence. Universal consciousness has no opinions and accepts whatever notions are suggested to it. It unquestionably accepts anything that our unbalanced mind presents at face value. Is it any wonder the world we live in, paying constant homage to human intelligence, is awash with conflict, disease, and misery? The Christian story of the Virgin Birth, repeated in many other mythologies, illustrates pure consciousness, the Divine Mother of all, Mother Nature, un-violated by the human mind, giving birth to the Christ Consciousness. With yoga, we're putting the mind in its place, still allowing it to add up our pocket change and direct the making of a peanut butter sandwich, but not permitting it to hog the mike and drone on endlessly with all its half-baked opinions, desires, and fears.

Bringing conscious awareness into the Nidra state we can receive healing and integration every time, just by being there. We also have the opportunity to exercise intent. We can use that accepting nature of Universal Consciousness to exercise our will. This is why Yoga Nidra was taught in the past to only the most proven initiates. It gives us the power to create reality, so be aware of the possibility of unintended consequences. This is a great responsibility and must be handled with discretion. Remember the old adage, "Be sure you really want what you ask for."

> "I am a weight that pleases me."

At the appropriate time, guiding you in your Yoga Nidra, I'm going to ask you to mentally state an intention. Give this some thought now—something you would like changed for the better. When forming an intention, state it in a way as if it were already a reality. Examples: "I am a weight that pleases me." "I am healthy and the condition I was suffering from is cured." "My sister and I love each other and the misunderstandings we had no longer exist." At a specific point in the directed Yoga Nidra experience I'm about to guide you through, I'll suggest you bring your intention forward in your consciousness. In the mean time just relax, but make a commitment to yourself to maintain alert awareness. Completely let go and follow my words without judgment or reservation. Relax because there is no way you can do Yoga Nidra wrong. Even if you fall asleep for a moment you are still receiving benefits. I've had us arrange the mats this way so if a person next to you does fall asleep and starts snoring, you can gently nudge them so it won't be distracting to others and will help that person refocus their awareness. Let's give silent permission now to the persons next to us to helpfully touch us if necessary.

> Energy
> follows
> attention.

If you need to shift your sitting position to be comfortable, do so now. Relax and breathe softly. Close your eyes and focus your attention between your eyebrows and about three inches in, the Third Eye. Follow your breath and gently gaze back and through the Third Eye. Relax. Energy follows attention. Listen to my voice. I'm going to read a prayer.

PRAYER

I open my heart to explore the divinity that is inherent within my body and my being.

I respect and honor my body as the temple of the Divine.

I am not just this body, but am the embodied spirit itself.

I am not my thoughts or my emotions.

I am witness to all that is in passing.

When I step into Yoga Nidra, I step into sacred territory.

I take this moment as an opportunity to transform all that holds me back from living in the light of the being that I am.

I let go of the limitations that I continually discover are held in my physical, mental and emotional bodies and keep me from realizing the divine potential inborn within me.

During this entire practice of Yoga Nidra, I make a firm commitment to apply myself one hundred percent.

I engage my full attention and non-judgmental awareness to fully surrender to the experience of the moment and the sacred union of body, mind, heart and soul.

Open your hearts and join me in a continuous OM. Ahhh Ohhh Ummm. Ahhh Ohhh Ummm. Ahhh Ohhh Ummm. Ahhh Ohhh Ummm. Shantay.

Focus your attention on your Third Eye, relax completely and let me be your guide. Instantly drop from your thinking center to your feeling center and from your feeling center, you will automatically transition into your being center.

> Drop all expectations.

Relax…

This Yoga Nidra is a process of learning to establish communion with your higher self. With your mind you can communicate with language. With your body, you communicate through the five senses. But to communicate with spirit, you have to go beyond what can be perceived through the mind and the body. So the most important thing entering into this experience of Yoga Nidra is to drop all expectations. It is all about learning to empty your mind of all tensions, all expectations and anticipations and opening yourself to 'what is'. And when you are totally open to what is, this is true communion. You have no disturbances coming from what it 'should be'. No reactions coming up, no mind, no hesitation, no doubt– none of those mental things. So dropping expectations is the dominant awareness. If thoughts come up, observe them and let them float by. Once you've established yourself on the deepest level of receptivity, which is also the deepest level of relaxation, it becomes the medium for you to receive directly from your higher power. When you are relaxed, your mind is quiet. You have entered into a non-doing state, and when you are doing nothing with your mind, your body or your emotions, you naturally drop into the deepest level of relaxation. You don't have to do anything, just follow my guidance to bypass your mind, to bypass your effort. You don't have to do anything or achieve anything. Renounce doer-ship. That's what Yoga Nidra is all about. When I guide you in the first part, through the movements and breath, the deliberate part of Yoga Nidra, do the movements and the breathing as I guide you, but with no striving. It can't be done wrong. Everything we are doing is just to help us enter into a relaxed state. There can be no fault with your performance, no reason to be anxious. Be at ease. You can do no wrong, create no tension, because everything is intended for relaxation. It's not about perfecting your practice; it's about relaxing through the practice. Shantay. Peace.

While you are sitting, breathing softly and maintaining an inward focus with your eyes closed, I'll guide you in a neck exercise. Sit up straight and relax. We'll do a few neck rolls to relax the neck and shoulder area. Keep the neck in alignment with the chest and inhale fully, and exhaling, gently press your head towards the chest. Be aware of any resistance or tension, not choosing for or against, just being aware of its presence. Inhaling, release to upright center. Exhaling, relax the neck to the right shoulder. Again take notice of any sensation in the area. Inhaling, bring the neck upright, back to center. Exhaling, slowly press the head to the back. Noticing any pull or tension in the back of the neck or top of the shoulders, breathe into it, relax the muscles around the area, and let go. Inhaling, come back to center. Exhaling, extend the head to the left shoulder, slowly feeling the stretch. Just bring your awareness there, observe, and let go. Inhaling, bring the head back to center. Exhaling, bring the chin to chest. Continue inhaling and exhaling, repeating the four movements, gently rolling the head.

> It's about relaxing.

And reverse…and repeat. Do several repetitions, rolling the head both directions.

Now that you've completed the movement, sit up straight and contemplate the sensations and energy flowing in your body. Bring attention to the Third Eye.

Now we'll do a seated Forward Bend. Extend your legs in front of you. Press the heels out and down with your feet close to each other. Extend the arms overhead. Inhale and extend up through the fingers and the crown of the

YOGA NIDRA

head. Exhale and press the chest forward, hinging at the hips, extending the torso forward and down. Arms are alongside the ears, but it is fine to put your hands on the floor near your hips if you need to support your lower back. Move the hands towards the ankles or feet. If you can, take hold of the feet. Do not pull or force. Breathe fully into the sensations that arise in the body. Extend from your lower back. Let the stretching be deliberate, non-aggressive and continuous to move you beyond your usual habitual limits.

> Discover the subtle layers of tension. Feel fully... let go.

Pull the abdomen in and extend the chest and torso further forward. Move deeper into your body and discover the subtle layers of tension. Experience the release of trapped energy. Be deliberate as you move deeper into the experience. As you exhale, relax your head and lower your forehead towards your knees. Use breath to help you open your body fully and melt away stress in all its forms. Allow yourself to feel fully.

Let go of any fear or expectations from your past performance. Relax and go further. To release, extend through the spine, arms and fingertips. Rise up slowly with arms extended overhead, palms facing each other. Extend your arms out in front of you and lower your palms to your thighs. Close your eyes and relax into pure sensation.

Breathe fully and let go more deeply with each exhalation. Let your mind be deeply engaged and absorbed by the dynamic energy flooding through your whole body. Relax, and create an open psychic space for the energy field to expand and grow. Feel it flood the entire body. Energy follows attention… nurture it.

Now we'll do spinal rocking and relieve any tension in your back. With eyes still closed and attention on the Third Eye, bend your legs and clasp your hands underneath the knees. Inhale as you rock back, and exhale as you rock forward. Do this several times until you are asked to stop.

Pay close attention to every sensation that comes and goes. Leave your mind and enter more fully into the sensations in the body. Relax. Stay out of your thinking center and stay in your feeling center. Feel the sensations.

Stop rocking back and forth and rest on your back, still holding your knees to your chest. Gently rock your hips from side to side and breathe into any resistance felt in the body. Relax and let go…

Breathe deeply, and let go even more.

Extend your legs out in front of you and relax. Let your whole body melt into the floor. Release any holding anywhere in the body. Become aware of the energy that has been released. Merge into this ocean of energy. Let it flow into any resistance, physical, mental or emotional, bringing you into the deepest state of balance and relaxation.

(Pause.)

Without too much disturbance, adjust your body in a comfortable position. Allow your legs to go apart enough to release any tension in the hip joint.

Now I'll guide you through palming of the face. Relaxed, with your eyes closed, bring your hands together and rub them vigorously, creating heat. Bring your palms to your face and gently massage your eyes…your eyebrows, (stay connected to your feeling center)…your forehead…temples, (massage fully until you release all the tensions)…jaws…your ears…your neck. Now take your hands and softly wipe your entire face with both palms. Feel the tension melt away under the healing touch of your palms and feel all the related tensions everywhere in your body disappear. Place your fingertips on your eyelids with the entire surface of your palms touching your face. Drop all expression from your face. Take a deep breath and let go…take another deep breath and let go…

> Merge into this ocean of energy.

Take your hands away from your face and lay them by your side, comfortably, with palms up, dropping into deep tranquility.

Now direct your full attention to your breath. Just naturally observe your breath, use the breath to release any tensions. Slowly deepen your inhalations and exhalations. Let your breath flow in a steady, uniform, unbroken stream.

Breathe deeply, but effortlessly. Let your attention be totally connected to your own breath as it flows in and out. Track the entire passage of your breath, going in, going out…Bring all of your awareness to the expansion of your abdomen as you breathe deeply in and out. I want to see the movement of your abdomen and chest as you breathe deeply but effortlessly. With each exhalation, release all tension held in your body. Release all expectations. Let go. Breathe out any tension held in the body. Feel it, feel yourself letting go. Each time you breathe out, empty your mind of any expectations; empty your mind of expectation and empty your body of tension. Feel exactly what is happening.

> ## Connect with visualization… with affirmation.

Connect what you are sensing in your body with visualization, with affirmation. Use your breath to progressively enter a deeper level of stillness and silence. Now relaxing even further, follow my guidance.

We will continue with five more very slow, very deep relaxed breaths. Count them like this: 5, I am breathing in…5, I'm breathing out…4, I'm breathing in…4, I'm breathing out…pause. Start at the beginning and continue until asked to stop. Be absorbed in the sound of your own breath. Let yourself be more relaxed and peaceful with each breath.

Stop counting and allow your breath to return to normal. Relax. Feel the energetic impact of breath as it is manifesting in your body as pulsations. Go into your body, feel it. Experience it. Let your mind merge and meld into it. Your awareness allows the energy field in the body to grow and expand. Relax and experience it. Energy follows attention. Let your mind melt and merge in the river of energy flowing through your body.

I will guide you into the next phase, to enter into deeper and subtler levels of relaxation—through a combination of sound and breath. I will demonstrate the humming sound of a bumblebee, mmmm, with your upper and lower teeth lightly touching. By slightly changing the shape of your mouth, cause the hum to vary, maximizing the vibration in the skull. Place your middle fingers between your brows over your Third Eye and use your thumbs to gently close your ears, just enough so that you can still hear me. Rest the remaining fingers on either side of the forehead and face. Relax. Now I will demonstrate. Mmmm…Take a deep breath and follow me on the second repetition: Mmmm, mmmm. Continue (allow 2 minutes). Now stop… Bring your arms to relax at your side and be still.

Feel the vibrations activating and stimulating your entire skull and brain. Feel the vibrations move through the body. Pay attention as they move through the torso, through the arms, through the legs. Notice how the energy follows attention and how your attention feeds the energy. As you engage your attention more fully, the energy begins to intensify and expand more freely. Empty your mind completely into the energy field and merge into the experience of the energy body, holding you in complete stillness.

Now focus that attention and energy on the spot between your brows, the Third Eye.

Adjust your body in a comfortable position but do not fall asleep. Make a vow with yourself to not fall asleep and stay aware. Throughout this entire period remain relaxed and motionless, alert and conscious. Stay in touch with my guidance at all times. Now drop into the deepest state of tranquility and peace. Bring attention to the Third Eye and drop into deep stillness. Allow yourself to follow my guidance through awareness of different parts of the body as I guide you. In Yoga Nidra you are no longer limited by the boundaries of the body and mind. You have shifted completely from thinking and doing to feeling and being.

Do absolutely nothing from now on. Simply relax. Drop into the deepest state of tranquility, stillness and peace in the Brow Center. Now your consciousness is in direct communion with your energy body.

Bring your awareness back to my guidance as we move through different parts of the body. As I guide you from point to point, accept that the energy of your attention will activate these centers and release any blockages.

Now bring your undivided attention to 1 your Brow Center…2 the pit of the throat…3 your right shoulder…4 right elbow…5 right wrist…6 your right thumb…7 second finger…8 third finger…9 fourth finger…10 fifth finger…11 your right wrist…12 right elbow…13 right shoulder…14 the pit of the throat…15 left shoulder…16 left elbow…17 left wrist…18 left thumb…19 second finger…20 third finger…21 fourth finger…22 fifth finger…23 left wrist…24 left elbow…25 your left shoulder…26 the pit of the throat…27 middle of the chest…28 your right nipple…29 the middle of the chest…30 your left nipple…31 the middle of the chest…32 your navel…33 the middle of the pubic bone…34 your right hip…35 your right knee…36 right ankle…37 your right big toe…38 second toe…39 third toe…40 fourth toe…40 fifth toe…your right ankle…43 your right knee…44 right hip…45 the middle of the pubic bone…46 your left hip…47 left knee…48 your left ankle…49 your left big toe…50 second toe…51 third toe…52 fourth toe…53 fifth toe…54 your left ankle…55 left knee…56 left hip…57 the middle of the pubic bone…58 the navel…59 the middle of the chest…60 the pit of the throat…61 and back to the Brow Center, your Third Eye.

> Merge completely with this sacred space.

Bring your undivided attention to the spot between your eyebrows. Allow yourself to merge completely with this sacred space. Remain empty, empty of all doing, empty of all past. Be empty of future, empty of 'I am'. Feel that you have given yourself totally and completely to the higher power to manage and the higher power will respond to all your prayers and affirmations. In the Third Eye, all your intentions and affirmations are realized and fulfilled. With ease, establish your trust. Here, there is nothing to achieve. You have entered the domain of grace, with no judgment, with no time. Allow your self to merge into this space and be empty…empty of all doing, all past, all future. All that exists is now.

All thoughts dissolve. This is your place of integration and wholeness, faith and trust, union with the true self. Here, within the Third Eye, your intention and affirmations are actualized and fulfilled with effortless ease. Now is the time to manifest your intention. Manifest your intention in your silent consciousness now, three times. Feel your intentions merge and become one with your higher self. If you have self-defeating patterns or habits from which you want to be freed, make that your intention now. Now, be free of those self-limiting habits and patterns.

Allow your intention to go to the deepest levels of recognition with no hesitation. With complete assurance, know that your higher self recognizes, honors and accepts your intention. Have faith and trust that it has been heard and is being acted upon by the higher power of the true source within.

There is no need for you to do anything about it. Just relax.

Bring your attention back to my guidance. Allow your entire self to respond spontaneously and effortlessly to what I say.

I unconditionally align myself with the higher power that is the core of creation and everything in the universe.

I am released from my self-image to explore, expand and experience the infinite potential unfolding within me.

My source is silent stillness, the womb of creation for the fulfillment of my intention. Shantay. Peace. I rest in peace.

I am the observer, the witness, separate from my thoughts and emotions, thoughts and emotions that float by, come and go.

I hold no one responsible for all that has happened in the past. I am free and clear of all that has happened in the past.

I go to the source within that heals all conflicts and restores my health and peace of mind. (Repeat)

I go to the source within that heals all conflicts and restores my health and peace of mind.

I am at peace with myself as I am, and at peace with the world as it is.

I enter the healing abode of my heart and release my unresolved feelings of fear, anger, blame, and shame.

I experience heart energy as love, melting all unresolved physical, mental and emotional blocks held in the form of ill health, stress and tension in my body.

(Pause)

Know that you are not the same person that went into this experience. Something has happened to you. You are forever changed, and notice with wonder the fundamental shift that will express itself in every realm of your being.

Establish yourself firmly in faith and trust to receive the grace, protection and guidance of the higher self within you.

If there are areas that need healing, just bring your attention there and feel the power of this presence to carry out that healing.

The more often you go to your source, the easier it will be to return there and the longer you can stay there.

You have prepared the base from which you can carry out interactions with life and interpersonal relationships with the integrative power of love and the source within.

You are the emissary of light and love. Carry it everywhere you go and to everyone you meet.

(Long Pause)

With eyes closed, gradually move, as if you are waking from a restful sleep.

Bend your knees and pull them closer to your chest, rock sideways gently.

Take your time. There is no need to hurry. Then turn to your side and curl into a fetal position. Feel the safety, comfort and protection of the womb of existence. Oh! Sweet Mother…

Bring your attention into your awareness again. Change nothing.

Every time you find yourself in reaction, you are empowered to replace it with your intention.

Now you can gradually begin to sit up, with your eyes closed. Stay deep in this inner experience.

Regardless of what you consciously recognize has or has not changed, know that something deep within has shifted to connect with your intention.

Become aware of your body and bring a deep sense of peace and contentment with you as you bring awareness back to the body…

Notice…

HOW RELAXED THE BODY IS…

HOW SOFT THE BREATH IS…

HOW SILENT THE MIND IS…

HOW QUIET THE HEARTBEAT IS…

BE STILL...BE GRATEFUL.

Know that you can easily enter here again and again.

Now, gradually open your eyes.

JAI BHAGWAN

VICTORY TO GOD

A Kundalini Meditation as recorded the last days of January 1999, just before the Millennium Shift, in its original form. Complimentary audio at jewelinthelotus.biz.

THE SEVEN VEILS

The benefits of meditation are extolled without much conversation about the mechanics. This is one example of kundalini meditation, explaining how it is performed. In practice, each meditation is unique, reflecting the individual and her/his growth through contemplation.

> *The object is to move attention up the back in stages.*

The object is to focus the attention on the lower spine and to move that attention up the back in stages. The eight stages are chakras. The first chakra is at the base of the spine. The second is located on the spine behind the navel; the third on the spine behind the diaphragm; the fourth behind the heart; the fifth in back of the base of the throat; the sixth centered behind the eyes; the seventh, just above the top of the head. The eighth chakra is located above that.

Attention is maintained through visualization. This meditation is a suggested series of images to focus awareness in each of the chakras in turn. You are urged to accept them without prejudice. The images are to evoke contemplation within each stage and are drawn from a wide variety of sources. Hopefully you can utilize each image as a tool, inspiring insights, knowing the images are only tools and are not absolute. After accepting these images and exploring the thoughts they provoke, you'll want to create images expressing your own perceptions.

Attributes of each chakra can be experienced when centered and still with attention focused inward. It might be noticed, for example, that each area of attention is accompanied by a tone. That the tone becomes higher pitched as focus travels from the lower to higher chakras. Similarly, visualization of each chakra might be awash in a hue – the lower chakras with deep reds, then oranges, then yellows and up the spectrum as consciousness ascends the levels. This association can be explained by contemplating how we've come to understand nature works. Our very limited understanding of the universe shows that nature repeats herself, using the same solutions on ever-grander scales in the creation of our reality. By observing phenomena within the narrow range of our senses, knowing that we can visually perceive a very small part of the light spectrum, and are only physically equipped to hear a very tiny portion of the waves we call sound, we can carry our understanding beyond what we can personally experience, knowing that patterns repeat themselves. All energy expresses itself in waves. By observing and reflecting on the small portion of the wavelengths accessible to our physical sense organs, we can make assumptions about energy not so plainly perceived. A relationship becomes apparent between spiritual energy and energy on the physical plane. In tune at various levels, the wavelengths correspond or harmonize.

The physical evolution of the species on earth has a parallel pattern in the development of a human child in the uterus. A single cell divides into groups of cells that specialize into organs, nerves, bone, etc. Some cells specialize to become the ever more complex nervous system and brain, wiring and intelligence necessary to direct all of the cells. A similar pattern of increasing complexity and refinement can be observed when awareness travels up through the chakras, a condensation of our spiritual evolution.

An issue that should be discussed before we begin our meditation is fear. There may be unresolved anguish over the unknown, reservations about completely letting go, distrust or a feeling of vulnerability. It's helpful to remember the natural tendency of life in the universe to evolve to a higher order. By facing our fears we come to understand them for what they are and, in effect, defuse them.

Sit comfortably on the floor with legs crossed, back straight, arms relaxed, palms up, back of the hands resting on the knees, with index fingers curled in touching the thumb below the second joint. Relax and close the eyes, roll the tongue up and back against the roof of the mouth and breathe softly through the nose.

Focus your attention at the base of your spine. Establish a point of awareness in the blood and tissues, feeling energy accumulating and increasing like an electrical charge. The vital saltiness of your blood, so like the primordial sea from which life arose. The electricity is awash in the correct combination of chemicals and nutrients. A spark! The spark of life. A single cell is the point of your awareness; a living being receiving stimulus from its immediate surroundings through chemical molecular attractions and repulsions. Attracted toward what feels good, it avoids what is unpleasant. Sunlight streams through the salty liquid from above like consciousness streaming down. The cell can use this energy supporting its life, a sun eater. Basking in the sunlight of your mindfulness, this sentient being prospers, growing, stretching the bounds of its cell walls. This sensation of expanding wellbeing increases, becoming sensual. This sensuality radiates out from the point of awareness, pleasurably arousing the sex organs. The focus is upon a seed bathed in vitality. Joyfully, the seed sprouts roots to absorb the enjoyment. Energy converges on the lower spine and radiates out between the legs. The labia and testicles, flooded with awareness and blood, pleasurably take notice of themselves. As the awareness increases, so does the pleasure, further stimulating awareness. The seed gathers energy and splits, sending up a sprout as the waves of electrical pleasure radiate up the vagina and the penis becomes engorged with blood and starts expanding. The seed pushes its roots deep into the nourishment, drawing up fulfillment. Its stem pushes upward through the salty red liquid. The vagina opens, yearning with desire for more of the

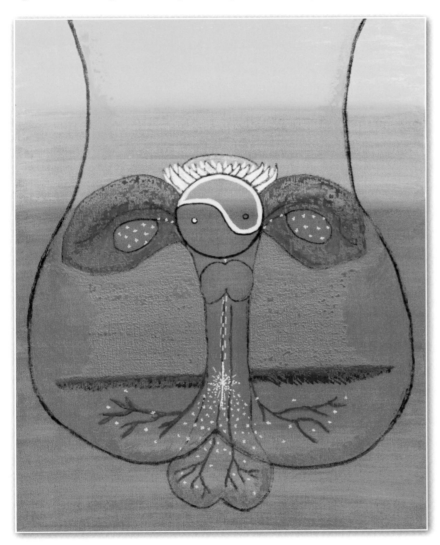

pleasure. As the penis swells, parting her lips, it moves deeper and upward into the warm wetness – the greater the sensation, the greater the ecstasy, the greater the focus. The vagina welcomes the engorged shaft until the intumescence parts the cervix.

Simultaneously the stem shaft of our plant breaks the surface of the water, basking in the warm orange light of the sun as it filters through the dawn atmosphere above. The plant stem opens, releasing two beautiful leaves that rest and bob on the water in the warm sunlight like the leaves of a lily. The water gently rocks the lotus leaves. The water below, the sky above. The vagina contracts, savoring more stimulation, causing the penis to throb with increased feeling. The vagina contracts in response, the penis swelling again with its good fortune. The two work together and against each other behind the navel, contracting and expanding. Duality exists in all its forms of expression: in and out; soft and hard; male and female; the relationship represented by the yin yang and either/or thinking. The one is made aware of itself through interaction with the other.

Sexual yearning intensifies; the waves undulate, rocking our lily. A carnal exclamation rises from the soul. All is beautiful lust as a tidal wave of passion breaks. The vagina pulls all creation in as the penis explodes, bursting with ecstasy. The union is complete. The two become three as great spurts of sperm splash mixing with the orgasmic cervical secretions and a wondrous blossom opens. A lovely lotus flower with a thousand white petals holds its face up to the sun. The sun looks down on the lily with warm rapture and the lotus follows the suns nurturing rays back to their source above and behind the diaphragm.

Sun – center of our physical universe, source of the energy that supports life on earth. The imagination floats up from the sun, out through the solar system, passing each planet in turn. Up ever further until we see the sun as only another star in a constellation of stars. Then the constellation recedes until it appears no more than a spot of light among billions of lights forming the Milky Way. Further out, until the galaxy appears but a tiny star among trillions of other galaxies, then outward to the edge of our universe. Looked at from the side, it looks like a little loop of energy.

Back down to the earth, we return with the speed of thought. Behind the diaphragm, our lily gently rocks on the water under the warmth of the sun. Dragonflies dart by, birds sing, and fish swim below the surface. What an amazing world. Attention microscopes down to a lotus petal. Down to the individual cells. Down further to the molecules making up the cell, then the atoms forming the molecules. Further down to the electrons, protons, and neutrons that comprise the atom. On down to the quarks that are the building blocks of the protons and neutrons. At this minute level, the distance between the matter that forms the subatomic particles is so great that it is, in its own scale, as great as the distance between the stars in the heavens. Our physical universe is mostly energy with very little matter. Further yet our imagination carries us, till we see what comprises the quarks, looked at from the side, little loops of energy.

The physical universe is so huge and vast, of which we know so little, but have the audacity to reduce in our minds to three dimensions: length, depth, and height. Simplistic conceptions are even more impaired attempting to explain the spiritual. Observing this physical plane and pausing to reflect on the wonder of the realm we inhabit, take a slow breath through the nose, counting to four as you inhale. Hold that breath for two counts of eight and then exhale to a count of eight. Ponder the Biblical expression, "God so loved the world that he sent his son"; translated, the spiritual placed itself in a physical form so as to be able to experience this amazing physical universe. When each child takes its first breath, a soul enters that body to utilize it for a lifetime as a vehicle to experience the physical plane. Forced head first into the world by the contractions of the birth canal, the newborn is lifted by its mother to her breast over the heart center.

Relax your breathing to its natural pattern, watching the young mother gazing down on the child suckling at her breast while the infant's hands idly grasp, feeling her hair. Experience love, the rhythm of the mother's heart beating through its four chambers. The cross, mystic symbol representing 'four', a crossroads. Time, the fourth dimension, carries the being through the experience of human love: mother, father, siblings, family, a warm puppy, a close friend. A crossroads is reached, emotion in an even higher form: awareness of God. With birth the individual travels outward through time from its starting point, in ever expanding circles of experience. At times we feel things are right, somehow connected and positive. At other times in our wandering, we have a sense of aloneness and feel out of sync and disconnected. It is as if a beam were shining down and we feel love when we're in its

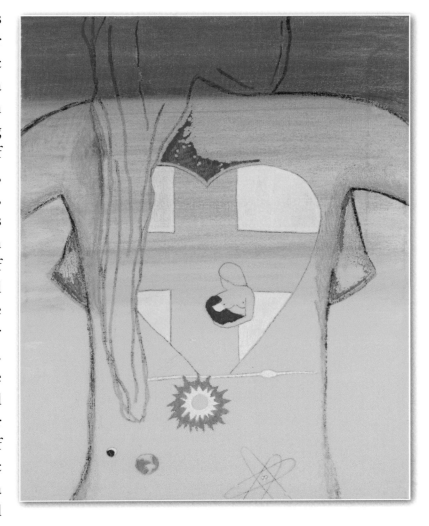

warmth, and loss when we're outside its light. The soul, traveling through its incarnations, circles ever further from its point of origin. As it gets closer to the source of the beam, the beam narrows and gets more dense. The distinction between being 'in' and 'out' becomes greater. The traveler no longer circles randomly, but through trial and error finds direction. With intent, a crossroads in development of the soul is reached. The Godhead is actively sought. God, divided into innumerable fragments, formed our existence. God, a part of everything. Now a piece of that everything discovers God in itself and seeks its way back to the whole. Numerous lifetimes of searching and we locate the exact direction to the source. No longer weaving 'in' and 'out' we have direction and we look out of the heart center up the spine to a star shining bright, guiding us as the Three Wise Men of Biblical myth were guided to an incarnation of the godhead extant on the physical plane. Visualize that star behind the throat. "I am the word, the way, the path." Effort is made to draw closer to the source of all pleasure, understanding and meaning. Other worldly pursuits aren't abandoned, but are now seen as tools for learning lessons that will help us draw closer. Knowing the true origin of all good, effort becomes efficient as the illusions of human politics are exposed. Many paths, some more appropriate to each individual's circumstance, offer real freedom. Any situation can be utilized. No sadness, because all souls return eventually to their source. No status, no completion. When compared to the backdrop of infinity, we're all only beginning. Ultimate love, where everybody makes it, no one is lost, all come home. What we'd deemed sin is mere dallying on the way. Our efforts are less important than the sincerity with which they are performed.

We feel those efforts being watched from above. That attention is followed up the spine to its apex behind the eyes, to the third eye, seat of consciousness, observing all whether awake or asleep. Seeing not just what's going on, but what is behind what is happening; not only what we do, but the thoughts and motivations that direct our acts. A coincidence, the homonym 'I' and 'eye'? Awareness, ever vigilant, where to hide from God (from our self) with every act and thought observed? Take a moment to be aware of the tone, the vibration that has followed your awareness up the spine, getting ever higher in pitch. Glance down the back to the starting point at the base of the spine and experience the energy flowing upward with that awareness. The sixth dimension, the pinnacle of intellect, summit of human experience, cusp of the physical plane. Each level of our development has its own seductiveness and we must not become too enthralled with the illusion of our cleverness. The siren of the intellect prompts the mystical concern that we can be trapped at the numerical crown of our narcissism, the sixth chakra.

Coarse energy flows up the spine, becoming ever finer, accumulating at the top of the head, tickling the pituitary. This finer vibration rises, floating though the crest of the skull. The bone of the skull acts as a barrier to the body below. Imagine a crescent moon, consciousness on the dark side of that moon, blocked from the light of the dynamo of the physical realm, the sun. During a solar eclipse the heavens appear hundreds of times brighter, simulating our ability to inhabit this realm closer to God. When God is described as being without sin, it is without the false concerns and limitations of the physical plane. To occupy that higher realm we must put the things of the world behind us. Our efforts don't merit our entrance. Admission is a matter of grace.

Think of this seventh dimension as an altar where spiritual energy, processed up through the chakras, is offered to the Divine and accepted with unqualified love. The intensity of that acceptance, or love, further stimulates the spiritual oscillations, further refining them, causing their ascent. Imagine love so great, our concept of love doesn't begin to approach it: completeness, understanding, beauty and joy so transcendent, it surpasses our cognition.

As on the physical plane, a food chain exists with higher life forms taking sustenance from lower life forms. This is the reason for our being, the answer to the meaning of life. Through the efforts we put forth achieving spiritual growth, we refine coarse vibrations into finer energy, nourishment for the gods. The Higher Powers become aware of an individual providing a substantial amount of refined vibrations and actively assist that individual towards their own benefit.

Consciousness beyond the sixth level is completely a matter of grace. All the seeker can do is place an offering of sincere efforts at the feet of God and humbly wait in awe for the Divine to elevate awareness. It is helpful to think about the greatness of the Higher Power within our limited capacity to perceive that which is so much greater than ourselves. The spiritual invitation is to sing praises to the Lord. A natural law comes into force: lower life forms' inability to perceive forms greater than themselves. We are analogous to the beneficial bacteria existing in our digestive tract. Those bacteria are totally dependent on us, the host, for life, but unable to perceive the host other than the bacteria's interaction with the small world of their immediate surroundings, an inability to see around corners in a curved universe. The most understandable form of physical energy, sound, because of the slowness of its wavelengths, illustrates the curvature of the physical universe. Do Re Me, a half-step and a curve Fa, So, La, half-step and a curve Ti, Do. The octave is the pattern taken by all forms of energy. Our senses just don't have the ability to perceive that pattern in light, spiritual, or other forms.

The aura permeating this highest level is an electric neon violet purple. Focus on the hue, listen to the prevailing tone and bask in the Divine. Feel total love and acceptance, knowing this is a perfect universe that is so vast, with so many dimensions, that we can only begin to perceive a most minute portion. It is terribly egocentric to think somehow we, humans, are the peak of evolution. In the vastness of the universe, worlds innumerable support what life forms? The diversity on this small planet is so huge, and existence is so varied and miraculous.

We cannot perceive those beings spiritually advanced beyond us, but knowing nature's tendency to repeat herself, can we draw broad assumptions? This human 'father face' we assign to the Higher Powers is but spiritual shorthand. Mere children spiritually, we use comfortable symbols to express what we intuit. What we consider God, these entities advanced compared to us, are they evolving too? What higher forms constitute their gods? Given what we can see in our small universe, wouldn't that seem to be the case? One octave flows into another and that into yet another, energy evolving in perpetuity. Creation–ever changing, ever growing, in a joyful dance to the Absolute.

There is no reason to reject the myths and language of your upbringing in a false show of sophistication. Embrace them for their power to share. Inspect them for the underlying truths that have become confused over time and telling. Often the opposite of the common interpretation may be real. A great teacher such as Christ tells us he isn't God, but human like us, his brothers and sisters, who are all children of God–only to have us deify him. Seek and you shall find. So many teachers with so much to illuminate–examine and find truth for yourself.

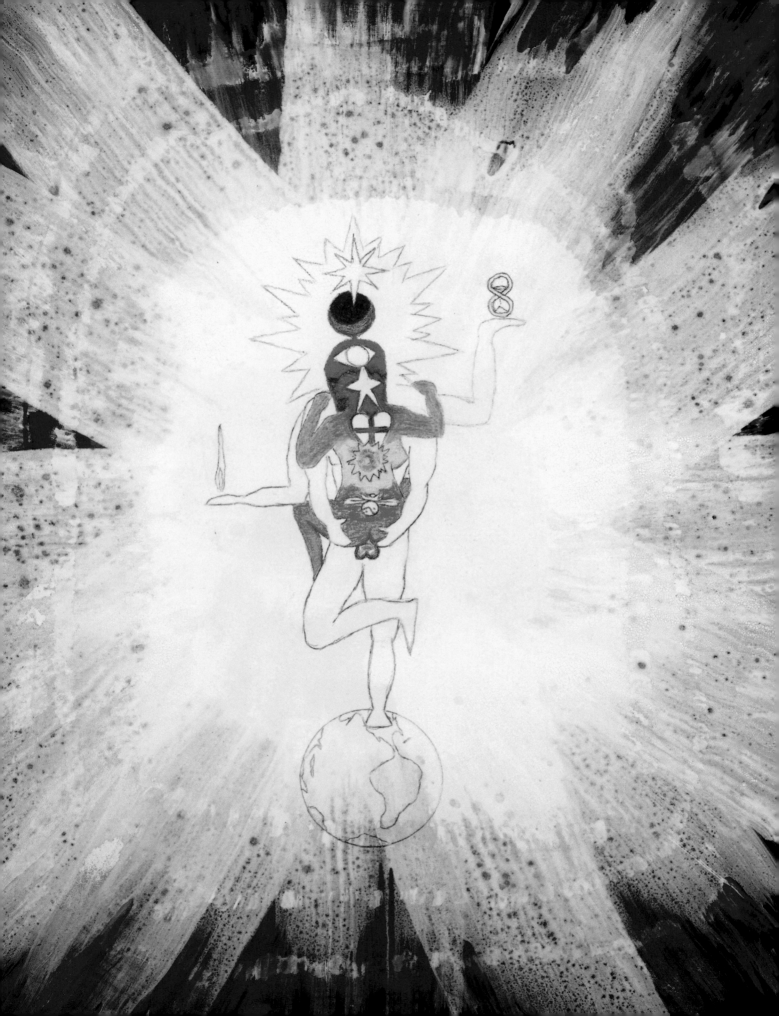

HOW THIS BOOK CAME TO BE

I might seem an unlikely person to have authored this book, but I feel my whole life has been preparation for the task. I haven't done everything there is to do wrong, but I have done enough that my life story seems incredible to most people. However, even when I was living wild and on the edge, even at my most desperate and confused moments, a part of me always knew that some underlying purpose gave meaning to existence and that we are all here to learn. Even before I was intentionally on a spiritual path, my outlook towards life has always been predominantly spiritual.

My first freedom as a young adult of the 1960's included all of the radical experimentation that era has come to represent. I started commercial fishing in high school and embraced that adrenaline-stoked, often epic, lifestyle. I spent much of my time in Alaska, in part because that was where the fish were, but largely because of the Wild West atmosphere. For many years, I tried to get a handle on my drugging and drinking, but my behavior had gone way beyond my control. Finally, at the very edge of complete self-destruction, I was able to give up alcohol, drugs and tobacco with the help of what Alcoholics Anonymous deemed my "Higher Power."

Having dropped the habits that kept pulling me down, apprehensions dissolved and new vistas of comprehension opened. I gradually started realizing a better self that had always been, but only now could shine forth. I was still living and working in Alaska as a commercial fisherman, but my head and body were clear of addiction. Several years later, I owned and operated a one hundred fifty-two foot tender. During the salmon season, another fishing vessel collided with my boat, which sank. I moved to Seattle to wait for the court hearing that would determine fault and liability. During that stay, a friend took me to a yoga class. The teacher was Marie Svoboda of the lineage of Sri T. Krishnamacharya who encouraged yogis to bring the teachings of yoga to the West.

Marie singled me out in front of the beginning yoga class–my first formal yoga instruction– and announced she wanted me in her advanced class. "You're strong and have spirit," she commented before the whole class. The friend who had taken me to that first class had been a student of Marie's for some time and she was so pissed that I was given special attention that she never attended another of Marie's classes. I tell people I was Marie's most inept advanced student in the final years she taught formal classes.

Marie was a Czechoslovakian ballerina before traveling to India where she learned yoga. She was strict and demanded that her students get it right, especially at first, to lay the foundation. Many of the first time students took it personally and didn't come a second time. Maybe this was an intentional weeding out process on her part, but if you could stand the heat of her attention, she was an exquisite teacher. I've never met anyone else who could diagnose a human body and could give direction on how to heal like Marie. She taught me so much about my body. I reflect on her with love every day as I recall her lessons.

I don't remember thinking of myself as overweight when I started learning yoga. I had gradually gained a few pounds each year. I was definitely not the 150 pounds I was as a competitive swimmer in high school, but I remember being upset when an old buddy asked me if I weighed 200 pounds yet. Once, when my wife was describing me to a friend of hers on the phone (unaware I could hear her comments) I was perplexed when she said I resembled the famously portly tenor, Luciano Pavarotti.

I went to yoga classes two to three times a week and I lost 35 pounds the first year without even trying. I was (and still am) able to eat enough to sustain several people. After a while, whenever another man who could stand to lose some weight showed up at the yoga studio, Marie would say, "Don, you talk to him." Gradually I got the message, but by that time I was becoming another, slimmer person.

Many people have told me they are the lightest they've ever been, and feel the best they've ever felt when they practice yoga. If you do yoga regularly with a group of people, you can watch them transform. This applies both to people who are just starting their practice, and to people who have done yoga for years, who seem to go on to ever-finer levels of beauty. It is not superficial. Rather, it is a peeling away of the meretricious constructs that cover the perfect expression of Divinity that is our true nature.

It has been twenty-six years now since I quit drinking. I live a peaceful, joyful existence and I'm in the best health I've known during this lifetime.

Recently I attended an organized yoga class and observed something I had seen before on many occasions. In the back corner of the studio, a young woman who was severely overweight was bravely trying to participate in the class. She was a beautiful person in her young twenties with flawless skin and perfect features, but she weighed probably twice what she healthfully should. She had difficulty with the postures and struggled to keep up. My heart went out to her. I admired her courage and knew yoga could do her so much good. I appreciated the dilemma of the instructor who had to keep the class flowing. I sadly realized the young woman probably wouldn't return, and might give up on yoga for life. I couldn't stop thinking of the tragedy of the situation. Reflecting on this event motivated me to write this book.

How many people feel they are overweight, out of shape, or simply shy about starting yoga surrounded by slender people who already know what they're doing? We all have to start somewhere. This book is a testament to what yoga has revealed to me, an ordinary guy. It acts as a bridge for those inhibited or needing some preparation before the fun of doing conventional group yoga classes. Traditionally, most yogis practiced alone. The instruction is designed to be complete enough that a person can do a lifetime of yoga by following the suggestions just in this book. By practicing yoga, you will experience an intrinsic understanding of the form your personal transformation should take.

If you practice yoga, even without focusing on weight loss, weight loss may occur if your body is carrying extra weight. An extremely thin person may gain weight. Imagine what can happen when we identify and utilize the processes that cause the body to seek its most perfect, natural physical expression? The yogic philosophy has an understanding of our bodies and the universe they inhabit that extends beyond the scope of our current popular science and medicine. We can use these insights to accelerate the realization of our ideal form. This form is coiled inside each of us, anxiously waiting to be released.

A person can do a lifetime of yoga by simply following the suggestions in this book.

When I started methodically observing the relationship between the philosophy of yoga and weight loss, I showed my notes to a friend who is a medical doctor. He said, "I think this could be an important book." As I spoke with friends about turning the emerging insights into a publication, they saw the importance of the undertaking and the good it could do. Like a crew that comes together for a commercial fishing venture, a few friends started to contribute their time and talents. William Wickett, a fishing partner in the past, is an accomplished photographer. His wife, artist Cecilia Wickett, teaches figure drawing. He photographed all the postures and paintings and she did the line drawings. My pretty niece, Marlow Mercer, demonstrated the postures. A dear friend I met during Yoga Teacher Training, Nelda Danz, edited the text. Michèle Savelle contributed her graphic design expertise to the book's layout, cover, and website. Klaus Liebetanz recorded the audio portions of the project in his studio. Sheryn Hara of Publishers Network helped navigate the final course of the voyage.

We are captain and crew on this enterprise. Now we ask to moor in the calm, peaceful harbor of your awareness.

SUGGESTED READING

These entries are arranged in alphabetical order, and no order of importance or ranking is intended. The notes in gray italics are not from the book's author or publisher, but are comments from this author. It is suggested selections be made intuitively, based on what attracts your interest.

Desikachar, T.K.V. The Heart of Yoga. Rochester, Vermont: Inner Traditions International, 1995. *Develop a personal practice while exploring the philosophy and traditions of yoga.*

Ellis, Peter Berresford. The Druids. Grand Rapids, MI: William B. Eerdmans Publishing Co, 1994. *The Celts and their priests, the ancient Druids.*

Feuerstein, Georg. The Yoga-Sutra of Patanjali. Rochester, Vermont: Inner Traditions International, 1979. *Translation and commentary.*

Fields, Rick. Chop Wood, Carry Water. New York: Jeremy P. Tarcher, Inc., 1984. *A guide to finding spiritual fulfillment in everyday life.*

Greene, Brian. The Elegant Universe. New York: W. W. Norton and Company, 1999. *Explores the Unified Field Theory through the lens of Superstring Theory to illustrate how mathematicians and physicists understand the universe.*

Gurdjieff, G.I. Beelzebub's Tales to his Grandson. London: Triangle Editions, 2006. *The early 20th Century metaphysician's impressions of "Everything" as related on a spaceship voyage returning to the Absolute.*

Heinlein, Robert A. Stranger in a Strange Land. New York: Putnam Publishing Group, 1961. *Science fiction which explores themes of individual liberty, self-responsibility, sexual freedom, and the influence of organized religion on human culture.*

Hoeller, Stephan A. Gnosticism, New Light on the Ancient Tradition of Inner Knowing. Wheaton, IL: Quest Books, 2005. *An understanding of Gnosticism and its reemergence through the ages.*

HOLY BIBLE. The New Testament and the Old Testament in various translations and printings.

Iyengar, B.K.S. Light on Yoga. New York: Schocken Books, 1979.
Yoga postures demonstrated in photographs with accompanying instruction.

Jacobs, Alan. The Essential Gnostic Gospels. London: Watkins Publishing, 2009.
Translations of some of the Gnostic Gospels.

Johari, Harish. Chakras, Energy Centers of Transformation. Rochester, Vermont: Destiny Books, 2000. *An exploration of Indian yoga that focuses on the psychic chakra centers.*

Johnson, Linda. Complete Idiots' Guide to Hinduism. New York, NY: Penguin Press, 2002. *Despite the unfortunate title, a most comprehensive introduction to Hinduism.*

Kaminoff, Leslie. Yoga Anatomy. Champaign, IL: Human Kinetics, 2007.
Anatomical drawings of yoga postures.

Neihart, John G. Black Elk Speaks. Albany, NY: SUNY Press, 2008.
Spiritual message of Oglala Sioux Holy Man as recorded 1932.

Schucman, Dr. Helen. A Course in Miracles. New York, NY: Foundation for Inner Peace, 1975. *A channeled metaphysical thought system on remembrance of God's love.*

Shah, Idries. The Way of the Sufi. London: The Octagon Press, 1980.
Account of ancient Sufi teaching.

Swami Rama. Living with the Himalayan Masters. Honesdale, PA: Himalayan International Institute of Yoga Science and Philosophy of the U.S.A., 1979.

Tolle, Eckhart. The Power of Now. Vancouver, Canada: Namaste Publishing, 1995

Tolle, Eckhart. A New Earth. New York: Penguin Press, 1998. *Living in the present.*

Yarbro, Chelsea Quinn. Messages from Michael. and More Messages from Michael. New York: Caelum Press, 1979. *Non-theistic spiritual doctrine revealed through channeling.*

Yogananda. Autobiography of a Yogi. New York: The Philosophical Library, 1946.

NAMES OF THE POSTURES IN THE TEN-MINUTE WORKOUT

By photo number:

30 Mountain Posture

31 Rocking Forward on Feet

32 Rocking Back on Feet

33 Making Arches

34 Lift Big Toe

35 Lift Other Toes

36 Right Angle Knee, Ankle Rotation

37 Bent Knees, Lower Body Rotation

38 Body Rotation

39 Forward Bend

40 Start of Angel Posture

41 Middle of Angel Posture

42 Top of Angel Posture

43 Elbows Up and Hands Turned Out Stretch

44 Elbows Up Twist

45 Reach Back, One Arm Up, One Down

46 Neck Roll

47 Half Moon

48 Flat Back Earth Diver

49 Windshield Wiper Knees

50 Windshield Wiper Legs

51 Spine Circles

52 Half Boat

(Continues on the next page)